To Missy,
a true Professional
and one who has
been an inspiration
To me.

Garland Ohng

1 - 13 - 2017

Sociolosophy:
Different Ways of
Thinking and Behaving

Sociolosophy:
Different Ways of
Thinking and Behaving

By Garland Sharp

Garland Sharp
130 Mockingbird Lane,
Oak Ridge, TN. 37830

Ordering Information:
Quantity sales. Special discounts are available on quantity purchases by corporations, associations, and others. For details, contact the publisher at the address above.

Printed in the United States of America

ISBN:153316441X

First Edition

Photo Caption

ACKNOWLEDGMENTS

I would like to express my appreciation for the unceasing love and support of my wife, Mildred. Many thanks go to Dr. Daryl Green whose guidance and support were there when I needed them. Words of appreciation are also owed to a true friend, Dr. Rosanne Smith, for her encouragement, support, and criticism of this book. Thanks also go to Dr. Rob Schriver, Ms. Barbie Scates, Ms. Astrid Brynestad, and Mr. Charles Slay for their support. Special thanks go to my editor and designer whose understanding and support played a great part in this effort. Thanks also go to my good friend John Mason who put the final touches on this book. Finally, I would like to express my appreciation to James L. Christian and Ian Robertson because their books changed my life.

Table of Contents

Introduction

> Every culture has devised its own way of responding to the riddle of the cosmos... there are many different ways of being human.
>
> *Carl Sagan*

Sociolosophy: Different Ways of Thinking and Behaving deals with improving the human condition in a world where individuals adopt many different ways of being human. This book's basic premise stems from the notion that individuals can better understand and improve their lives through new ways of thinking, feeling, and behaving. It explores the concept that individuals' definitions of themselves and their world determine their thinking, feelings, and behaving (TFB) characteristics. It outlines methods for developing TFB-characteristics that individuals might use in developing themselves and their understanding of life which works best for them.

The truth might be defined as our view of reality. Truths which successfully worked for us in the past might fail to work successfully for us, in the present. Truths which work for one person might fail to work for another. For example, if we are Christians, we adopt truths which work for Christians — such as the virgin birth, the burial, and resurrection of Jesus Christ, along with a host of other Christian beliefs. In contrast, if we define ourselves as a Muslim, we would adopt truths which work for Muslims — such as Allah is God, and there is no God but Allah, along with a host of other Islamic beliefs.

Although Christians might consider Islamic beliefs false, and Muslims might consider Christian beliefs false, they believe that their religion is true. Their truths work for them. They take action according to their truths or beliefs. When Christians pray, they expect and believe that they receive answers from God. In contrast, when Muslims pray, they expect and believe that they receive answers from Allah.

This book emphasizes that each of us can define and redefine ourselves and our world. When we accept external definitions or define ourselves and our world, we adopt truths which may or may not work best for us. For example, in Knoxville, Tennessee, your

Figure 1 The Milky Way. As individuals respond to the riddle of the cosmos, they find many different ways of being human.

Figure 2 If you are Muslim or Christian, only parts of this book may be true for you.

author observed that a doctor in his office wore a nice white lab coat, black slacks, and polished shoes; while outside this office, a poorly dressed man who appeared to live on the street passed by the window. The apparently successful doctor and the apparently unsuccessful street person had defined themselves and their worlds differently. The apparently successful doctor may or may not have been happy, but it is for sure that unless the street person was delusional, he was not happy. For whatever reasons, each adopted a unique set of truths to suit their lives. The street person's definition of self and his world differed from the doctor's definition.

This book examines why some people, such as the doctor, find apparent success and happiness while others, such as the street person, live in misery. This book examines the effects of individuals' beliefs on their actions and how their beliefs can act as internal controls which greatly influence the likelihood of them feeling successful or not. It also deals with the many external factors which contribute to determining their level of success or failure.

This book deals with different ways of thinking and behaving. It considers different ways of being human. It outlines ways people can change, to overcome their internal and external controls. It explores how people develop, maintain, and change themselves and their world. It examines the importance of people's definitions of themselves and their world — and the truths which support these definitions. It suggests methods which people might use to identify the need to create and maintain changes in their lives.

Many people accept and internalize the reality presented to them without performing a critical evaluation of that reality. Then, they suffer passively. This book examines the notion of individuals using **Sociolosophy** to develop truths which work best to empower them.

Figure 3 The Street Person vs. The Doctor
What makes the street person a street person? What makes the doctor a doctor? There are many different ways of being human.

I do not feel obliged to believe that the same God who has endowed us with sense, reason, and intellect has intended us to forgo their use.
Galileo Galilei

Figure 4. Philosophy, An Introduction to the Art of Wondering and Sociology.

One might ask, what is *Sociolosophy*? It is the critical analysis of human behavior by examining both the social sciences and philosophy to provide additional insight into how we develop, maintain, and change our thinking, feeling, and behavior in an attempt to devise better ways of being human.

Although Sociolosophy involves other disciplines, it is heavily influenced by the works of philosophy and sociology by James Christian and Ian Robertson respectively. James Christian wrote the book entitled *Philosophy, An Introduction to the Art of Wondering*. Ian Robertson wrote the book entitled *Sociology*. Although the books were written by different authors on different subjects, when they wrote about a particular topic they generally agreed and reinforced each other's writings. These books helped to re-shape your author's life. As a result, he chose the word Sociolosophy to use in the title of this book.

Sociolosophy attempts to blend ideas from many disciplines to develop a workable philosophy which individuals may use to improve themselves and the human condition. Psychology helps to explain human behavior and mental processes. David Myers' book entitled *Psychology* provides valuable information from this area. History helps to explain how and where people's beliefs and ideas originated. Religion helps to understand the powerful influence that beliefs have on human behavior and our understanding of reality. Therefore, *Sociolosophy* intertwines ideas from sociology, philosophy, and other areas to provide a framework which may prove valuable for living.

Individuals might use the ideas presented in this book to redefine themselves and their world, to discover truths which work best for them. They might use the ideas to understand themselves first, and then understand the cultural patterns and conditions which help in developing the self. They then might adopt and maintain new TFB-characteristics embracing different ways of being human, which could prove beneficial.

As you become clearer about who you really are, you'll be better able to decide what is best for you — the first time around.

Oprah Winfrey

PART ONE

LEARNING TO BE HUMAN

Chapter 1

The Self and the Human Predicament

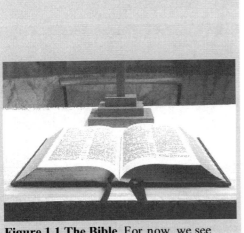

Figure 1.1 The Bible. For now, we see through a glass, darkly. 1 Corinthians 13:12

At every moment, our behavior is determined by our genes, our experiences, and personalities.

David Myers

As people choose to begin the journey of redefining themselves and their world in order to adopt better and more satisfying ways of being human, they need to understand the "self." They also need to identify problems and question assumptions that stand in the way of them developing and maintaining autonomous selves. The self is your distinct way of being human based on your unique characteristics. The self is the conscious being who experiences the world. The self includes a physical component, the "being," and a mental component, the "experiencing." Therefore, in this book, "self" refers to your total being, which includes both physical and mental components. In other words, the self is your distinctive way of being human.

From our hereditary blueprint and our environment, we develop our thinking, feeling, and behaving characteristics. These unique TFB-characteristics coincide with our personality. We experience life based on our personality — our distinct TFB-characteristics. We act consciously and unconsciously based on these characteristics. The TFB-characteristics, or personality, form the basis of the self. Therefore, we might change either by changing our TFB-characteristics, which will change the "self" or by simply redefining ourselves and then adopting TFB-characteristics which support the new "self."

Much of the self appears to result from learning. Based on our hereditary blueprint, we become who we are through interactions with the environment, including social interactions with others. Our hereditary blueprint consists of the genes that heavily influence our physical and mental characteristics. Therefore, our hereditary blueprint and our environment determine and maintain the "self."

Our heredity blueprint may limit our potential in some areas, such as our ability to grow taller or to achieve success in certain areas, but the environment might determine whether we reach our potentials. For example, heredity influences individuals' skin color and height. If they live in a hot climate, and they do not have enough food to eat, they could become darker and shorter. People can be born with the potential for high achievement, but never achieve success. For example, many people with the capacity for high achievement are imprisoned. Not only does success depend on the environment in which we live, but our response to that environment. We might live in an environment filled with wealthy and successful people, and never become wealthy or successful.

The self appears to be unique to humans, or at least different for them. If we look at other biological systems, we can find many similarities to humans. Some animals, such as the chimpanzee, resemble and can be taught to act like humans. However, individuals

Of all the wonders of the universe, the greatest is man.
Aristotle

It is the large brain capacity, which allows man to live as a human being, enjoying taxes, canned salmon, television, and the atomic bomb.

G.H.R. Von Koenigswald

are capable of thinking at higher levels than other biological systems. They have the freedom of choice, while other biological systems follow their instinct. Unlike other biological systems, humans think, plan, worry, and decide on different courses of action. They have the capacity for abstract thought and reason. Generally, they have a moral sense of right and wrong. They believe in gods and believe that they have souls.

Although research suggests that animals have some thinking abilities, they do not think on a level with humans. Myers stated that "the most tangible indication of our thinking power is language — our spoken, written, or gestured words and the way we communicate them as we think and communicate." Humans certainly use language and think at a higher level than animals. It appears that humans are fully self-conscious, and experience distinct personal identities or selves far beyond other biological systems.

Figure 1.2 Chimpanzee and a Chimpanzee's Painting. Research suggests that one of our closest biological systems might have thinking abilities. A chimpanzee accomplished the painting on the right.

After a general understanding of the self, individuals need an understanding of certain human predicaments which they face. There are certain predicaments or inescapable conditions, simply resulting from being human. Because of these conditions, individuals do not know all that is going on in the world. They come to know what they know based on limited and sometimes distorted information.

Time presents one such predicament or inescapable condition. The American Heritage College Dictionary defines time as "a non-spatial irreversible continuum." Time has no space, always continues, and is irreversible. Neither the past nor the future exists. Only the present exists. Individuals can only exist in the present time.

They find themselves in the inescapable condition of being trapped in a single occurrence of time.

Space causes another inescapable condition. Space is where things physically exist, where individuals exist in the present time. Therefore, we find ourselves trapped in a single time and a single space. Not only are we trapped in this egocentric trap of a single time and space, we are also trapped in another inescapable condition which Ralph Barton Perry described as the Egocentric Predicament. Each of us is trapped in the physical organism called our body, and we can only experience the world through our perceptions. To further complicate matters, we have to deal with our Reticular Activating System (RAS). This part of the brain filters information and allows information to be detected and perceived, limiting what we experience. The RAS causes us to detect from the environment only essential or relevant items at any particular time. We develop scotomas — or blind spots — to the non-essential. Therefore, each of us has egocentric or selective detection. This is the process of selecting only portions of what we are capable of observing, for use in thinking. We focus our attention on the things which we feel are essential for thinking, at each point in time. The perceived non-essentials, at the time, are ignored or filtered out.

We also have to deal with our subconscious minds. Sigmund Freud believed that the subconscious mind — sometimes without being known by individuals — causes them to think, feel, and behave irrationally. The subconscious mind determines to a large degree each individual's TFB-characteristics. Therefore, it influences how we think, feel, and behave.

As though being trapped in the inescapable conditions including the subconscious mind pushing us into irrational behavior were not enough, to make things worse, we have to deal with our conscious mind. Based on limited information, many of the beliefs held by the conscious mind limit our thinking. Therefore, what we know has varying degrees of plausibility or certainty. What we know is only a representation of real world objects/events. Therefore, we should be very careful with what we "know" to be true.

After discovering what constitutes self, and knowing that we face certain inescapable conditions simply by being human, we each must also recognize and understand the culture and the TFB-characteristics which we have accepted. If we recognize and understand these, we can decide whether to change, discard, or accept and conform to the culture and TFB-characteristics of our society.

We should be very careful with what we "know" to be true.
Garland Sharp

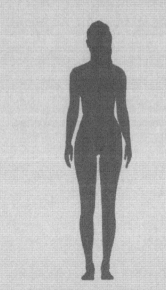

Figure 1.3 Individuals find themselves trapped in a single time and space. They also find themselves trapped in the physical organism called the body.

Therefore, we should seek to understand and recognize the TFB-characteristics and culture we have accepted, before we attempt to redefine ourselves and the perceived world.

Figure 1.4 Sigmund Freud. Freud believed that the subconscious mind, in ways sometimes unknown to us, causes us to think, feel, and behave irrationally.

Free 3D Business Men Marching Concept by lumaxart, thegoldguys.blogspot.com/Wikimedia Commons/CC-BY-SA-2.0

Figure 1.5 If we understand and recognize the culture and TFB-characteristics we have accepted, we can decide whether to change, discard, or accept and conform to the culture and TFB characteristics of the society.

Chapter 2

TFB-characteristics: The Path Toward Being Human

Adolf Hitler

Vanessa Sharp

Figure 2.1 These two individuals were socialized to become quite different people. Hitler, one of the most infamous men in all of history, compares poorly with Vanessa Sharp, who became a valuable addition to the world.

Individuals enter the world with few or no beliefs, and without their TFB-characteristics firmly established. At birth, they do not believe in Jesus or Allah; they do not believe that they are superior or inferior, nor do they believe that there is an Easter Bunny. Yet, they may — over time — be made to believe any of these. As Christian profoundly stated, "We know that individuals can be acculturated into any set of customs, beliefs, and values; they can be made to believe, value and even worship almost anything." Through the continuing process of acculturation or socialization, social interaction causes us to acquire our thinking, feeling, and behavior characteristics — as we learn how to be human.

The acculturation or socialization of individuals occurs primarily through conditioning, observational learning, and language. Although we might learn in other ways, these three intertwine to cause much of our socialization to take place. Things which we detect and perceive in our environment forms the basis for learning. Through the process of sensation, transducers such as the eyes, nose, and ears detect physical energy from the world then encode it in the brain. Through the process of perception, individuals interpret or decode the sensations, forming information.

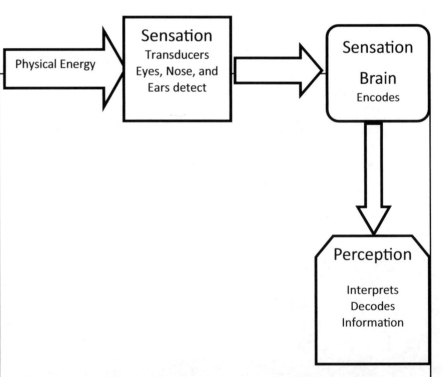

Figure 2.2 Sensation & Perception. Through sensation, the transducers detect physical energy, and this is encoded in the brain. Through perception, the sensations are decoded, and information is created. Two individuals might be exposed to the same thing, but they are almost certain to detect and perceive it differently.

People start life basically with a clean slate and their unique hereditary blueprint. From birth, their environment and hereditary blueprint, including the inescapable conditions of life, aid in determining what they detect and how they perceive what is detected from the environment. They develop TFB-characteristics or personalities based on what they detect and perceive. They create beliefs or mental concepts to represent reality. These mental constructs might not always have a high degree of accurate correspondence with real world objects/events. The TFB-characteristics then aid in determining what and how individuals detect, perceive, and react to future events from the environment. Each person might build a belief system quite different from others. Two individuals might be exposed to the same thing but detect and perceive it differently.

From birth, in part because of our unique hereditary blueprint and the inescapable conditions, we have selective detection and biased perception (SDBP). As discussed earlier, we cannot detect all that is going on in the world — partly because of being trapped in a single time, space, and body. Also, through selective detection, we tend to detect from our environment only the things which are essential or relevant to us at the time. Our hereditary blueprint and TFB-characteristics aid in determining what is relevant or essential. We also face biased perception and interpret things differently based on our hereditary blueprint, and pre-existing beliefs.

Based on our TFB-characteristics and hereditary blueprint, we interpret the world differently. Because of the egocentric predicament, we can only experience life through our perceptual and information processing equipment. Therefore, selective detection and biased perception or SDBP is the process of selectively detecting and perceiving — with bias — what is going on in the world. What we experience does not exactly match the real world object/event. Using SDBP what we experience is based on our sensation and perception. We develop and cling to TFB-characteristics based on our SDBP.

Our instinctual quest to stay alive, and our hereditary blueprint, (because we have few or no beliefs at birth) initially aid in determining what we selectively detect and how we perceive — with bias — what is detected from our environment. Then, our established TFB-characteristics and our hereditary blueprint influence the detection and perception process as we experience the environment. This acts as a chain reaction. Through SDBP, the child's or the youngster's existing beliefs aid in shaping the development of new beliefs.

After individuals adopt a belief, the feedback selectively detected and biasedly perceived from the environment may tend to reinforce that belief. Therefore, people do not detect or perceive their world apart from SDBP. Because of SDBP, things perceived to exist or not

A human being always acts, feels, and performs in accordance with what he imagines to be true about himself and his environment.

Maxwell Maltz

to exist in the environment are represented in personal knowledge. Things which are not essential to the person at the time, such as injustices to other groups, the person might fail to detect and perceive that they exist. In contrast, things could be non-existent in the environment but believed to be essential to the person at the time (such as witches causing illnesses), the person might detect and perceive that they exist. In this way, SDBP causes people to build elaborate belief systems quite different from one another, and some will be far from accurately representing real world objects/events.

What we detect and perceive in our environment forms the basis for learning. As stated earlier, although other factors might exist, we form personality and learn the ways of society primarily through conditioning, observational learning, and language. During socialization, classical and operant conditioning aid in forming individuals' TFB-characteristics or personality.

Classical conditioning occurs when a neutral stimulus produces a conditioned response, with Pavlov's dogs as one of the most famous examples. Ivan Pavlov used classical conditioning to condition dogs to salivate. He sounded a tone and then fed the dog. After repeatedly sounding the tone then feeding the dog, Pavlov discovered that when he sounded the tone, the dog salivated with or without feeding. Pavlov had conditioned the dog to salivate when the tone sounded. The tone acted as the stimulus which produced the response, the salivating of the dog, in expectation of the reward, the food.

Individuals can be classically conditioned. A patient might have an illness, and a doctor gives the patient red pills ... and the pills cure the illness. If repeated several times, the doctor might use red placebo pills to cure the patient. The doctor conditions the patient to believe that the red pills cure illnesses. If a woman nearly drowned as a child or has been raped, she might be conditioned to become afraid at the mere sight of a body of water or being alone at night. We find ourselves conditioned to react to stimuli in the environment, aiding in forming our personalities or TFB-characteristics.

Operant conditioning occurs when the feedback from an act causes the individual to repeat or avoid the action. Myers stated that one could distinguish classical from operant conditioning by asking the following questions: "Is the organism learning associations between events that it doesn't control (classical conditioning)?" or "Is it learning associations between its behaviors and resulting events (operant conditioning)?" Operant conditioning works, in part, because people tend to repeat acts that bring about desired results and avoid acts that fail to bring about desired results.

Feedback in the form of reinforcement and punishment aids in conditioning people. Reinforcement increases the desired behavior and punishment decreases the undesired behavior. Reinforcement in

Figure 2.3 Pavlov used classical conditioning to condition dogs to salivate.

the form of rewards or the removal of adverse conditions and punishment works because of people's propensity to move toward pleasure and move away from pain. If people stray from a predictable path, reinforcement and punishment cause them to get back to where they belong. For example, parents provide their children reinforcement to increase desired behaviors and punishment to decrease undesirable behaviors. In this way, parents use operant conditioning to raise children.

Elephant trainers train elephants to remain captive through conditioning. The elephant handler places a chain staked in the ground, attached to one of the baby elephant's legs. As the baby elephant struggles, it is unable to free itself. As the elephant continues to struggle to free itself, the elephant's efforts fail to bring about the desired result, and the elephant stops trying. It now believes — which is true — that it is unable to free itself. The baby elephant has acquired learned helplessness, the feeling of helplessness caused by things beyond its control. When the elephant grows larger and stronger, it could easily free itself from the chain or any small cord that the elephant's keeper decides to use. Yet, the elephant remains captive believing it is unable to free itself. The elephant now associates the small cord or chain with being unable to free itself. The trainer has conditioned the elephant to remain captive.

Another example of conditioning is that of a dog that belonged to the Sharp family. When a puppy, the kids kept the dog inside a fence. After the puppy repeatedly tried to jump over the fence without success, the puppy believed — which was true — that he was unable to become free. The puppy also acquired learned helplessness and stopped trying to escape. After becoming a large dog, he could have easily jumped over the fence, but he never tried. Like the elephant, conditioning caused the large dog to remain trapped. The dog associated the fence, as the elephant associated the chain, with being unable to become free. This shows the power of conditioning on animals.

Humans must deal with conditioning as part of the human condition. They might find themselves conditioned as the elephant and the dog to remain trapped in undesirable conditions and live far below their potentials. Through operant conditioning, after repeated failures, individuals might acquire learned helplessness and stop trying. Through classical conditioning, the mere presence of obstacles, whether real or imagined, might cause individuals to be fearful and expect failure. They have conditioned responses to stimuli, real and imagined. Internalized self-limiting beliefs through conditioning cause them to remain trapped in undesirable conditions, and respond negatively to feedback from the environment.

As the dog and the elephant, people can be conditioned even to

A domesticated bull elephant in Thailand by OxOx from Oxford, UK, Wikimedia Commons/CC- BY-SA-2.0

Figure 2.4 This large elephant associates a small cord or chain with being unable to free itself because of conditioning. Without conditioning, the elephant would easily free itself.

12

the point of being institutionalized. A lady in Cookeville, Tennessee who had a daughter who had been incarcerated for many years, described "institutionalization" as the condition prisoners find themselves in, after being incarcerated for long periods. She stated that they became more comfortable in prison than in free society. If institutionalized, when the time comes for their release, they might break the rules to remain in prison. If released, they might break the law to return to prison or commit suicide because they cannot cope with being free in society.

These individuals feel uncomfortable living in society as free individuals. This did not only occur with that lady's daughter. Your author's brother spent most of his life incarcerated. If released from prison, he did something to get back where he thought he belonged. He found more comfort in prison than living free in society. As prisoners, many individuals find themselves institutionalized in the lower stratum of society. Being institutionalized or conditioned for the lower stratum causes them to stay in their comfort zone, the place or state where they feel comfortable.

Just as the full-grown dog and the elephant — without the conditioning — could easily have escaped, many individuals' conditioning causes them to remain trapped as impoverished, uneducated, or prisoners. They become institutionalized. The institutionalized situation becomes their comfort zone. They find some comfort when they remain there, although their comfort zone might bring many discomforts such as living in poverty in America — or in an extreme case like living as outcasts in India. If they move from their comfort zone, the stress alone, without any external influence, might cause them to move back to that comfort zone.

During socialization, observational learning also aids individuals in forming their TFB-characteristics and aids them in learning the ways of the society. Through detection and perception, they learn from observing their environment, which includes observing others. Much of what they learn about self and the world comes from observing and imitating others. Because of this, we can find several generations of unwed, publicly assisted mothers or wives of abusing men. These people learn these negative behaviors by modeling others in their environment. In contrast, we can find several generations of successful entrepreneurs. These people learn positive behaviors by modeling others in their environment. Observational learning intertwined with conditioning causes learning to take place for people. Through observational learning and conditioning, they learn by observing and then doing. They learn by trial and error. They learn by trial and success.

This leads to another form of learning. Some learning is obtained through people's experiences. These experiences might come from

Figure 2.5 Conditioning can make people feel more comfortable in prison conditions than when they are free. They can become institutionalized.

In the heating and air conditioning trade, the point on the thermostat where neither heating nor cooling must operate — around 72 degrees — is called "The Comfort Zone." It's also known as "The Dead Zone."

Russell Bishop

doing things which were not observed. This type of learning along with conditioning causes new learning to take place for them. If they find that the action has positive consequences, they might repeat the action. In contrast, if they find the action has negative consequences, they might avoid the action. However, individuals do learn by observing others, then imitating or avoiding the observed behavior. Through conditioning, what they observe in their environment might cause them to avoid or adopt certain behaviors. For example, if they watched their friends being hanged in the town square for stealing, they might become fearful at the thought of stealing and avoid that behavior. They might avoid marriage if they observe their friends getting divorces.

People may imitate a behavior if it brings rewards and fortunes for others. They might take up stealing if their friends become rich by stealing. They might get married if they believe their friends are happily married. Through observational learning and conditioning, if the observed behavior brings pleasure to others or the person after adopting the behavior, this reinforces the behavior. In contrast, if the observed behavior brings pain or punishment to others or the individual after adopting the behavior, this dissuades the behavior.

Individuals also obtain their TFB-characteristics and learn the ways of society through language, the media of written, spoken, and gestured words. Without language, the age of communication known today would be impossible. Without language, any society would find great difficulty in surviving. Through language, each generation can build on the successes of past generations. The stories told, books read, classes attended, television shows viewed, and the web pages visited all use language to cause learning to take place for individuals. People also use words from their language, along with images, for thinking.

People express their experiences through language. Therefore, language certainly influences thinking and beliefs. People also learn through gestured language. A mother can communicate with a child through gestured language without speaking a word. A shepherd may communicate with a Border Collie through gestures. Although other methods exist, individuals obtain personality and learn the ways of their society primarily through conditioning, observational learning, and language.

Figure 2.6 If we watched a friend being hanged in the town square for stealing, we might become fearful at the thought of stealing and avoid stealing.

Chapter 3

Socialization:
The Internalization of Reality

Socialization is the internalization of reality which may or may not accurately match real world objects/events.

Garland Sharp

Each society has agents to socialize or acculturate people to have the TFB-characteristics of that society. As stated earlier, through the process of acculturation or socialization, individuals — through social interaction — acquire their TFB-characteristics and learn how to be human. This determines what they believe are right and acceptable behaviors in the society. They become a part of the society, and this enables them — and the society — to survive. The socialization agents socialize or acculturate individuals to establish, maintain, and sometimes change their TFB-characteristics … usually in an evolutionary fashion.

The four primary socialization agents are the family, the schools, peers, and the media. The socialization agents provide conditioning, models for observational learning, and language that aid in developing individuals' TFB-characteristics. The primary socialization agent for individuals, starting at birth, is the family. The family usually has the most influential effect on a person's TFB-characteristics, because each individual depends on caregivers for many years. We usually establish our first emotional bonds with our caregivers, as we start to learn the TFB-characteristics of the society. The early environment, mainly created by our parents or caregivers, provides the initial conditioning, models for observational learning, and language that aid in our early development.

Figure 3.1 The family teaches the child to adopt certain acceptable behaviors and to avoid other unacceptable behaviors.

The family teaches us to adopt certain acceptable behaviors, and to avoid other unacceptable behaviors. The family teaches us certain beliefs or concepts — including some which are intended to be temporary such as the Easter Bunny, Santa Claus, and the Tooth Fairy. Other beliefs or concepts are intended to be permanent, like God, loyalty to country, and two plus two equals four. The family, which includes the parents and caregivers, begins the process of socializing individuals with personality and the TFB-characteristics of the society.

I learned the way a monkey learns—by watching its parents.

Queen Elizabeth II

The school aids in further socializing the individual. The school reinforces some of the things which the family teaches. The schools socialize people with certain skills, knowledge, and attitudes to aid in helping the individual and the society to survive. This helps to hold the society together. The books read, and the classes attended aid us in developing the TFB-characteristics of the society. For example, the American school system socializes children with the culture norms and values of America. The school focuses on teaching the English language, for example. The American School System teaches each child more American History, American Government, and more on the American way of life than the history, government, and the ways of life of other countries. The schools help to shape each person's personality. These schools teach us how to think and act like Americans.

Our peer groups also aid in socialization. Through conditioning, peer groups cause us to conform through reinforcement and punishment. The group conditions us to have desired behaviors and to avoid undesirable behaviors, based on the group's norms. Through observational learning, we observe and imitate. We adopt much of our language, habits, and behaviors from peer groups. We tend to talk, dress, and act like our peers.

The media aids in socializing us with the TFB-characteristics of the society. The media consist of the forms of communication using the written and spoken language that we receive in our environment. These media include such things as newspapers, radio, television, and the Internet.

The media teach people — including the family, educators, and peer groups — the society's accepted and unacceptable norms and values. The media communicate the established or changing norms and values of the society to individuals throughout the society. Television appears to be the most influential of these media. Because of the power of television to influence individuals' behavior, a thirty-second commercial during the Super Bowl costs millions of dollars.

Although the family, schools, peers, and media represent the four primary agents for socialization, there are others. Groups such as clubs, corporations, the military, and teams also aid in socializing or acculturating us to establish, maintain, and sometimes change our thinking, feeling, and behaving characteristics. These agents expect their members to act according to the groups' rules. As with the peer group, these agents condition individuals by giving positive reinforcement to the conformist and punishment to the dissenter. If individuals deviate from the rules, the groups try to get the deviants back within the group rules' boundaries. Whether the group is a

Education is a system
of imposed ignorance.

Noam Chomsky

Figure 3.2 The American school system aids in socializing children to the American way of life.

If you don't read the newspaper, you're uninformed. If you read the newspaper, you're mis-informed.

Mark Twain

gang, a church, or a club, it appears to be difficult for kids as well as adults to dissent from the norms of the group.

It takes a village to socialize a child.

Garland Sharp

The group often exhibits crab-like thinking. This kind of thinking might cause individuals to remain trapped in disempowering groups. We do not have to put a lid on a container full of crabs to keep the crabs from escaping. If one crab tries to climb out, the other crabs will prevent the escape. They will kill or bite the claws off the escaping crab to keep it in the bucket. They will drag the crab back down with them. In groups, often the members will do whatever is necessary to make its members conform to the rules and accepted TFB-characteristics of the group. In many cases, this is detrimental to members of the group, as well as causing the group to become stagnant and irrelevant.

The expectation of people to conform to the rules of the society is not new. For example, in Galileo Galilei's time, the Roman Catholic Church formed the Inquisition, a tribunal for discovery and punishment for people guilty of heresy. The Church hunted and delivered people believed to be guilty of heresy to the Government. The Government punished the people, sometimes by death or imprisonment. Giordano Bruno and Galileo spoke against the Church's teaching. One such tenet was that the Earth was the center of the Universe.

Figure 3.3 The peer group aids in socialization.

Figure 3.4 We do not have to put a lid on a container of crabs to keep the crabs from escaping.

They are playing a game. They are playing at not playing a game. If I show them I see, I shall break the rules, and they will punish me. I must play their game, of not seeing the game.

R.D. Laing

Smoke and Mirrors by Grea, Sangrea.net /CC-BY-ND-3.0

Figure 3.5 Socialization might cause false beliefs.

Because of their belief that the Earth revolved around the sun along with other beliefs which conflicted with the Church, Bruno was killed, and Galileo was forced to deny his beliefs and then placed under house arrest for the remainder of his life. People like Bruno, Martin Luther King, and Malcolm X were killed for not conforming to the TFB-characteristics of the society. People like Galileo, Nelson Mandela, and Rosa Parks were imprisoned for not conforming.

Galileo Galilei on trial   **Giordano Bruno**

Figure 3.6 Galileo and Bruno were punished because their beliefs contradicted the Church's teachings. Galileo was made to renounce his beliefs and then placed under house arrest for the rest of his life. The Inquisition had Bruno killed.

If people define situations as real, they are real in their consequences.
W. I. Thomas

As a man thinketh in his heart, so is he. *(Proverbs 23:7).*

The Bible

Through the process of socialization or acculturation, people can be made to adopt many different ways of being human. It does appear that we can be made to believe almost anything. We act in terms of our beliefs. Years ago, the American Sociologist William Isaac Thomas made an observation that is known as the *Thomas Theorem*. He stated that "If people define situations as real, they are real in their consequences." This observation was not new. Many years before Thomas, the Bible stated, "As a man thinketh in his heart, so is he." (Proverbs 23:7.)

Robertson affirmed, "If members of a society believe that the earth is flat, that Jupiter rules the heavens, that illnesses are caused by witches, or that there are such things as x-rays, then the supposed flatness of the earth, the rule of Jupiter, the presence of witches, or the existence of x-rays will become as much a part of reality to people in that society as any other feature of their social or physical world. They will act in terms of that reality — by not sailing toward the end of the earth, by making sacrifices to Jupiter, by burning witches at the stake, by avoiding or by making use of radiation." To further illustrate the Thomas Theorem, if a woman believes in ghosts, she might see ghosts. For example, your author's grandmother believed in ghosts, and she saw ghosts. In contrast, women who do not believe in ghosts do not see ghosts. If people believe in the flatness of the earth, they might not sail toward the supposed edge of the earth for fear of falling off the edge. If they

Figure 3.7 The Salem Witch Trail. If we believe that witches cause illnesses, we might have them killed.

Figure 3.8 Washington Allston's painting "Saul and the Witch of Endor." Some people might believe in witches because the account found in 1Samuel, Chapter 28 of the Bible reinforces that belief.

As a man thinketh, so is he, and his thinking might be far from real world objects/events.
Garland Sharp

Rationalism belongs to the cool observer. But because of the stupidity of the average person, they follow not reason, but faith. This naive faith requires necessary illusions and emotionally potent oversimplifications, which are provided by the myth-maker to keep the ordinary person on course.
Reinhold Niebuhr

believe that witches cause illnesses, they might have the witches put to death. If people believe that Jupiter rules the heavens, they might make sacrifices to Jupiter. Witches and Jupiter effectively become real for them.

As you might have recognized, there are truths perceived by people that are real, and there are truths which become real because people perceive them to be real. Real truths are true for everyone. For example, 2 + 2 = 4 and the fact that gravity causes dropped objects to fall to the Earth are true for everyone whether they perceive these as true or not. In this book, perceived real truths are truths which become real because people believe them to be real. These fail to be true for everyone. For example, the "truth" that witches cause illnesses is one of these.

Individuals find themselves acculturated or hypnotized with certain truths. Many of these might be considered perceived real truths. No place is this illustrated more clearly than with religion. The American Heritage Dictionary defines a myth as a "traditional story dealing with supernatural beings, ancestors, or heroes that informs or shapes the worldview of a people, as explaining aspects of the natural world or delineating the customs and ideals of society." Clearly, some myths might be based on real or perceived real truths. If it is traditional, the story may be defined as real and become effectively real in its consequences. Such a story can then become a religion.

This can be seen with the beliefs by billions of people in religions that have contained thousands of gods from A to Z throughout recorded history. People have believed and worshipped gods or goddesses from Anubis of Egypt to Zeus of Greece. We can see how many truths become effectively real because people believe they are real. People can be made to believe nearly anything. For example, Zeus, whom many people were made to believe in, was once the chief god of the Greek Empire. However, Zeus has no influence over people today because they have been made to believe in other gods.

People might conclude that most religions are myths based on perceived real truths except ***their*** religion, which is based on real truths. Therefore, they are atheists towards the many other thousands of gods and goddesses believed to have existed or believe to exist. Their god is the only true God. Again, individuals find themselves acculturated with certain beliefs which may be real or only perceived real truths. As Christian stated, "They can be made to believe, value, and worship almost anything."

Although some scholars disagree, it is generally believed by most that Constantine sanctioned Christianity in the Roman Empire.

Anubis

Zeus.

Figure 3.9 Billions of people have believed in gods and goddesses from A to Z. This proves that many truths become effectively true because people believe they are true.

When I told the people of Northern Ireland that I was an atheist, a woman in the audience stood up and said, "Yes, but is it the God of the Catholics or the God of the Protestants in whom you don't believe?"
Quentin Crisp

The religion of one age is the literary entertainment of the next.
Ralph Waldo Emerson

Most history books report that in 313, with the edit of Milan Constantine and Lyceum, rulers of Rome, stopped the government-sanctioned persecution of Christians. These history books also indicate that in 325, after becoming the single ruler of Rome, Constantine met with about 300 bishops at the Nicaean Council to determine the nature of Christ. The history books indicate that the council concluded that Jesus was God, and this became known as the Nicaean Creed. Whether we believe that the Nicaean Council dealt accurately with Jesus or not, had Islam had been around, and if Constantine had declared Allah as God, then Rome would probably have become an Islamic Empire. The Roman citizens would have started thinking and acting as Muslims. For them, instead of Christ answering their prayers, Allah would have answered their prayers. Many Christians today might have become Muslims, attending the Roman Islamic Church and believing that Islam is natural and right.

We can see that if people define a situation as real, the situation becomes very real in terms of its consequences. Robertson stated, "If our culture believes the earth is flat, or that cause and effect are related to magic, then it is through these concepts that we will interpret the world." As stated earlier, our established beliefs aid in determining our selective detection and biased perception. In many cases, we might find ourselves acculturated or **hypnotized** with beliefs far from real world objects/events — such as Jupiter ruling the heavens or flying teapots.

If our culture believes the earth is flat, or that cause and effect are related to magic, then it is through these concepts that we will interpret the world.

Ian Robertson

If, however, the existence of such a teapot were affirmed in ancient books, taught as the sacred truth every Sunday, and instilled into the minds of children at school, hesitation to believe in its existence would become a mark of eccentricity and entitle the doubter to the attentions of the psychiatrist in an enlightened age or of the Inquisitor in an earlier time.

Bertrand Russell

Bertrand Russell believed, as did James Christian, that people could be made to believe and worship almost anything. He believed that people could be made to believe that a flying teapot was sacred if it were affirmed by ancient books, taught as a sacred truth every Sunday, and instilled in the minds of children in schools.

The aphorism, "As a man thinketh in his heart so is he," not only embraces the whole of a man's being, but is so comprehensive as to reach out to every condition and circumstance of his life. A man is literally what he thinks, his character being the complete sum of all his thoughts.
James Allen

Conclusive proof of the Flying Teapot.

Figure 3.10 Russell's teapot. People can be made to worship almost anything.

Chapter 4

Being Hypnotized

> It is no exaggeration to say that every human being is hypnotized to some extent, either by ideas he has uncritically accepted from others, or ideas he has repeated to himself or convinced himself are true.
>
> **Maxwell Maltz**

You dreamt you were a hypnotist? Stock poster, ca. 1900 by trialsanderrors/ Wikimedia Commons/CC BY 2.0

Figure 4.1 While hypnotized, individuals will do strange things. Maltz believed that all humans are hypnotized to some extent, either by ideas, they have uncritically accepted from others, or ideas they have repeated to themselves or convinced themselves are true.

Maxwell Maltz, in his book entitled *Psycho-Cybernetics,* stated that everyone is hypnotized. The socialization or acculturation process seems to have a hypnotizing effect on individuals. We might believe that the word "hypnotized" incorrectly describes the acculturation of people. However, if India's society can acculturate an "outcast" within India to be an outcast, and pass this status on to future generations, hypnotism might correctly describe acculturation.

If America's society can acculturate a girl to be a poor unwed mother, and pass this status on to future generations, hypnotism might correctly describe this process. If people can be acculturated into any set of customs, beliefs, and values — and if they can be made to believe, value, and even worship almost anything, hypnotism might correctly describe the acculturation of individuals.

Although people are not in a trance-like state, their acculturation causes many of them to behave as outcasts, poor unwed mothers, or people who will worship almost anything. Maxwell Maltz stated, "You may have never been formally hypnotized. But if you have accepted an idea — from yourself, your teachers, your parents, friends, advertisements — or from any other source, and further, if you are firmly convinced the idea is true, it has the same power as the hypnotist's words over the hypnotized subject."

Hypnotists can cause individuals under hypnosis to do amazing things. The hypnotist can have them spell words or solve math problems they have never attempted in the past. The hypnotist can convince the subject to lift weights they never believed they could lift before. However, if the hypnotist told the subject that they could fly, the subject could not fly. If the hypnotist told the subject to jump from a tall building without being killed, the subject would still be killed if they jumped from the building. Therefore, the things the subject does under hypnosis are things that they and others are capable of doing anyway. This notion is extremely important and well worth remembering. Myers corroborated this notion when he talked about hypnotized subjects. He stated, "In experiments, their strength, stamina, learning, and perceptual abilities are like those of motivated un-hypnotized people."

Maltz also corroborated the notion that the things which people can do under hypnosis, they are capable of doing without hypnosis. He stated, "The powers that the hypnotist brings out in the subject were there all the time. They did not use these powers because they had been hypnotized to believe that they did not have the powers." He profoundly stated, "that it would be truer to say that the hypnotist had **dehypnotized** them than to say he had hypnotized them."

Maltz explained that people when told under hypnosis that they cannot lift a pencil from a table, they are unable to lift the pencil.

Because if he (Taylor), is a missing link, it means the Sacred Scrolls aren't worth their parchment.

Cornelius, Planet of the Apes

Drawn by Charles Slay

Apes avoided the Forbidden Zone

The Forbidden Zone

Figure 4.2 Sometimes the truth is in the Forbidden Zone.

They are no less strong under hypnosis, but the muscles of their arms work against each other causing them not to be able to lift even a pencil, for example. If they are acculturated to accept the TFB-characteristics of the society, these patterns have the same power over them as if they are hypnotized. They, as the hypnotized subject, are no less strong, smart, or worthy, but disabling TFB-characteristics cause them to work against themselves.

If acculturated to believe that the earth is flat, individuals avoid sailing to the supposed edge of the earth. They would only sail out so far and feel uncomfortable, then return to safety. We should ask ourselves, how much are we affected by such notions as flat world thinking. How far are we sailing? What have we been acculturated or hypnotized to believe about ourselves that keeps us trapped?

What are our forbidden zones? In the movie *Planet of the Apes,* the apes in power knew that in a certain area, evidence existed that proved humans had been superior to apes. The evidence — if discovered by the masses of apes — could have shattered the society's cherished beliefs in its history and religion. It would have made their sacred scrolls worthless.

As in any society, the beliefs in its history and religion help to give stability to the society. To keep the masses of apes from learning of the evidence about humans, the apes in power defined the location of the evidence as the Forbidden Zone. Because of the fear of the Forbidden Zone and the punishment from the apes in power, the masses avoided the Forbidden Zone.

Not being known doesn't stop the truth from being true.

Richard Bach

As with the masses of apes, our TFB-characteristics developed during acculturation or socialization strongly influence what we will or will not do. These patterns sometimes create self-fulfilling prophecies and self-limiting beliefs. Individuals act in accordance with their beliefs and feelings about themselves and their world. If they believe that they are incapable of achieving something, they might not attempt the thing, or if they attempt it, they might only give a half-hearted effort ... causing them to fail. By not attempting or by giving halfhearted efforts, individuals fail — thereby fulfilling the prophecy that they cannot achieve what they desire. In contrast, if people believe that they **are** capable of achieving or being something, they will try harder, quite possibly causing them to succeed.

Photo Caption

Therefore, **you** should become your own *dehypnotist* and dehypnotize yourself of false beliefs. You should rid yourself of false beliefs even if you have to enter forbidden zones and disrupt the society.

Men do not attract that which they want, but that which they are. Their whims, fancies, and ambitions are thwarted at every step, but their inmost thoughts and desires are fed with their own food, be it foul or clean.

James Allen

Our doubts are traitors, and make us lose the good we oft might win by fearing to attempt.

William Shakespeare

Chapter 5

Cultural Integration

There might be a good reason for the road less traveled.

Garland Sharp

Times Square, NYC

Frog Jump, Tennessee

Figure 5.2 An individual raised in New York City would be quite different if they had been raised in Frog Jump, Tennessee.

Although socialization or acculturation can be damaging for many individuals, it has its rewards. Without socialization, the society and the people would fail to survive. Socialization causes individuals to act in ways that hold the society together. Although no two individuals in the society have TFB-characteristics which are exactly the same, the diverse characteristics cohere and interact to help the individual and the society to survive. Even though the environment or the society is unique, the TFB-characteristics provide beliefs that interact to hold the environment or society together.

Individuals' heredity blueprints are given facts. They have no choice of their parents or ancestors. As stated earlier, based on their unique hereditary blueprints and the inescapable conditions, the environment causes them to have certain TFB-characteristics. All societies have specific TFB-characteristics that determine and maintain the individual's self and the society. These characteristics are considered natural and right in that society. Individuals often conform to these TFB-characteristics with little or no questioning.

The socialized TFB-characteristics of the society provide us with norms, values, and common beliefs acceptable within the society. Without these, the society could not survive. These general abstract concepts provide us with guiding principles for thinking, feeling, and behaving. For example, in America, people do not walk down the street naked. They should not steal from or kill others. In America, the society supports values such as patriotism, industry, and honesty. These norms, values, and beliefs help maintain stability for both the individual and the society.

Although the TFB-characteristics obtained through acculturation provide norms, values, and common beliefs in the society, people reared in the same society might be quite different. Each person is unique. No one has the same genetic blueprint or deals with the inescapable conditions in exactly the same way. In the same country, the culture or environment can be different and affect its members differently.

A person raised in New York City would be quite different if they had instead been raised in Frog Jump, Tennessee. Although more similar than if they had been raised in Iraq, the person would be quite different. In the same country, each environment has some specific TFB-characteristics unique to that environment. The people in each environment — such as a section of a country, neighborhood, or a home — have some TFB-characteristics considered natural, meaningful, workable, and correct in that environment. From house to house in the same neighborhood, people are different. The section of the country, the neighborhood, and individual homes promote similar thoughts, feelings, and behaviors that make them unique.

> If we speak a different language, we would perceive a somewhat different world.
>
> Ludwig Wittgenstein

Figure 5.1 As the shark, individuals conform to TFB-characteristics with little or no questioning.

The common TFB-characteristics provide consistency and predictability for individuals and the society. Again, if individuals with a particular hereditary blueprint were raised in a different country, they would be quite different. If they were raised in Iraq, they would probably speak Arabic, believe in Allah, and be Muslim. If they were raised in America, they would probably speak English, believe in Jesus Christ, and be Christian. Individuals raised in Iraq view the world and think somewhat differently than individuals raised in America. They have different beliefs or truths about many things based on their environment. The shared beliefs help to maintain the society.

Every society socializes individuals with roles that are needed for the individual and the society to survive. The society defines the roles. It also defines the norms and the rules for the roles. Most people accept the given roles and follow the norms and rules for the roles if the society is to survive. When most of the people in the society conform to the roles, chaos in the society is avoided. For example, the socialization agents such as the family and the schools socialize people to speak English in America. This adds cohesiveness to the society.

We come to know and expect certain things from ourselves and others in the society. Because of socialization or acculturation, we usually know the roles of others whom we encounter. We probably know how the next prostitute on the street, the next doctor in his office, or the next clerk at Wal-Mart will act. We know how our doctor, lawyer, or accountant will act. We want these professionals to be predictable. We want these professionals to act out their roles and provide the required services.

If a woman accepts the role of mother, she probably knows how mothers should act. The person who accepts the role of a car driver knows that the job has rules. People expect the next person they meet driving a car in America will stop at a stop sign or red light. They expect that person to be driving on the right side of the road. If driving in England, they expect the next person to be driving on the left side of the road. They want the drivers to be predictable.

The norms and rules for the roles make people predictable. After they follow the given norms and rules for a while, these become internalized. The norms and rules become habits. The habits make it easy for them to conform to the roles. This avoids chaos and allows the society and the individual to survive. However, some of the habits might be detrimental to people. As they accept definitions of themselves and their world, they accept the roles and rules ascribed to the definition causing them to be predictable. Problems might occur when people fail to accept the roles or follow the norms and rules of the accepted roles. The society could breakdown.

Socialization leads to conformity. Conformity makes individuals predictable. They know how they should act and how others should act in certain situations. Sometimes there is a good reason for the road less traveled. However, in many cases, socialization or acculturation limits individuals. They accept their given roles and follow the norms and rules of the roles, even when it is detrimental to them — such as accepting the role of an outcast, or an inferior black person.

People live their lives according to their roles and the rules for the roles. If this works for them and they find happiness, maybe no change is necessary. However, If our defined roles fail to work effectively for us, we might recondition ourselves to adopt more empowering roles. If we do not find good reasons to avoid the road less traveled, we might take that road and adopt roles that work more effectively for us. We might build our lives based on better truths or better definitions of reality.

Figure 5.3 The Tower of Babel of the Bible by Lucas van Valckenborch. Without a common language, towers remain unfinished.

Figure 5.4 If individuals do not find good reasons to avoid the road less traveled, they might take that road and adopt roles that work more effectively for them.

PART TWO

THE POWER OF THE TRUTH

Chapter 6

Truth— The Definition of Reality?

The truth is more important than the facts.

Frank Lloyd Wright

$$2 + 2 = 4$$

Figure 6.1 Real and Perceived Real Truths Some beliefs have a high probability of being true such as 2 + 2 = 4, and other beliefs have a low probability of being true such as the Easter Bunny.

As defined earlier, truth is the individual's view of reality. However, reality varies from culture to culture, from person to person. The TFB-characteristics of individuals based on their hereditary blueprint, the inescapable conditions, and their environment cause them to view reality differently. Their internalized thoughts, feelings, and behaviors determine their reality. As people allow themselves and their world to be defined, or as they define themselves and their world, they develop and perceive what is real to them.

There are many different ways of being human. As stated earlier, there are real and perceived real truths. As individuals obtain their beliefs through socialization, some have a high probability of being true such as 2 + 2 = 4, and other beliefs have a low probability of being true … such as the Easter Bunny. These beliefs or truths determine the "self" and govern behavior.

People will act according to their personal truths whether the truths have a high probability of being true or not. If people define situations as real, they are effectively real in their consequences. They will not sail to the edge of the Earth. They will kill witches, leave cookies for Santa, and wait for the Easter Bunny. Yes, if they believe that Jupiter rules the heavens, they might make sacrifices to Jupiter. In contrast, if they believe Baal rules the heavens, they might make sacrifices to Baal.

Most people in societies accept the given reality and act as if it is a real truth. If they allow others in the society to define reality, this reality shapes their evolutionary process, thus influencing what they become. People internalize the TFB-characteristics of their society and uncritically accept the reality which is presented to them. It appears easier for these people to accept the reality presented to them than to redefine themselves and their world. When the majority of people in any group accept the reality presented, it is hard for a single person to break away from that reality — even when conformity is detrimental to the person.

The movie "The Truman Show" illustrated this notion. The movie had several striking metaphors. Truman or "true man" was the only true man on the entire island where he lived. Everyone else on the island was either an actor or worker. Without him knowing it, Truman's whole life had been broadcasted on world television. Kristofferson, who resided in a big sphere in the sky, appeared to represent God metaphorically. He created, produced and controlled the show. When asked during an interview why Truman never escaped the island or found out the truth about his life, Kristofferson made a profound statement. If you take the time to read and really understand this statement, you might understand why you sometimes find yourself stuck in a negative situation. Then you can dehypnotize yourself from many self-limiting beliefs, compromises, and fears and

Figure 6.2 English: *The beggar by* José Ferraz de Almeida Júnior. Português: *A mendiga.* Many people accept the reality presented to them.

Question Reality!
Bumper sticker

The "self-image" sets the boundaries of individual accomplishment. It defines what you can or cannot do. Expand the self-image and you expand the area of the possible.
Maxwell Maltz

move toward a more autonomous self. Kristofferson stated that Truman never found the truth because "people **accept** the reality presented to them."

Even when Truman ceased to accept the reality presented, forces were in place that caused him to remain on the island. Everyone he interacted with tried to keep him on the island including his supposed parents, wife, and his best friend. Kristofferson, who appeared to represent God, also worked to keep Truman on the island. In the real world, sometimes everyone we interact with tries to cause us to conform to "the reality presented." It is hard for us to escape from the reality presented and to avoid conformity when people have their feet on our necks. In the movie, Truman's supposed family, friend, the other people on the island, and Kristofferson had their feet on Truman's neck. More importantly, Truman's foot on his own neck — or his self-limiting beliefs such as his fear of water and his belief that his world represented reality — kept him on the island for a long time. We might understand why people find difficulty in escaping "the reality presented" to them. They have to deal with their foot, the feet of others, and sometimes the big feet of gods on their neck.

Truman's truths or beliefs aided in keeping him on the island. As with Truman, our truths or beliefs keep us where we believe we belong. Our truths or beliefs determine our comfort zones. As stated earlier, if people get out of their comfort zone, stress occurs based on their beliefs. To eliminate the stress, many people just go back into their comfort zone. Therefore, their beliefs or truths greatly determine what they will or will not try, what they can or cannot do, or what they will or will not do. Henry Ford has been reported to have said, "If you think you can or think you can't, you are right."

For example, if a man believes that he cannot run a four-minute mile, he might never be able to run a four-minute mile. If we believe that we cannot do a task, and yet we accomplish that task, to maintain our sense of truth, our reticular activating system might filter out the accomplishment. We might rationalize why we accomplished the task. Through rationalization, we might blame the accomplishment on such things as luck or an accident.

Our self-image is our truth or beliefs about ourselves. It is how we view ourselves. Our self-image determines our self-esteem, or how we feel about ourselves. If we have a positive self-image and high self-esteem, it appears that we feel more worthy. With feelings of worthiness, we appear to be more inclined to accomplish or have what we desire. However, if we have a negative self-image, low self-esteem, and feelings of unworthiness, we might not try to accomplish or have the things which we desire. If we do try, we might give

I am opposed to million-aires, but it would be dangerous to offer me the position.
Mark Twain

Figure 6.3 George Bernard Shaw stated that the lack of money is the root of all evil.

a half-hearted effort ... and fail. The failure reinforces our established beliefs. The failure conditions us for further failure.

If leaders or mythmakers can determine our truths or beliefs, the leader or mythmaker can control us — or at least make us predictable. If mythmakers define our truths and convince us to have a negative self-image and low self-esteem, this will determine how worthy we feel. If we view ourselves as unworthy, we probably will not ... and many do not ... aspire to our full potential. Therefore, we should shed irrational beliefs such as unworthiness. Negative beliefs or truths such as unworthiness help to guide our thinking and behavior. Unworthiness might cause us to believe erroneously that something is bad or wrong.

If we find ourselves convinced that something is bad or wrong, we might avoid that thing — even if it is good for us. For example, some Christians adopt the belief that it is harder for a rich man to get into heaven than a camel to go through the eye of a needle. Some say the eye of the needle represented a gate. However, the needle being a gate does not matter. The statement illustrates that people who have riches will find it hard to get into heaven.

"It is harder for a rich man to get into heaven" is a convenience statement for the rich, who evidently do not believe the statement. If they believed the statement, they would rid themselves of their riches. The poverty-stricken individual might find the statement "it is hard for rich men to get to heaven" disabling.

Those people who believe that the possession of riches will make it hard to get into heaven ... will probably avoid riches. They believe that the riches might cause them to go to hell where they would burn forever. Forever is a long time! This kind of truth guides many of their actions, and these actions cause them to avoid wealth. People like these and their money are soon parted. Other individuals have the money, and these individuals find themselves stuck with empty bags.

If we continue reading the verses following the discussion of the camel going through the eye of the needle, we find that the Bible states that all things are possible with God. This is a more empowering statement for the poor person to adopt. This statement includes rich men going to heaven versus statements comparing rich men to camels going through the eyes of needles.

We might find it necessary to redefine money and the way we view money. We need to adopt the "truth" that money is neither good nor bad — no more than a building or a jacket is good or bad. These objects just exist. Therefore, we should strive to have wealth

Come Later

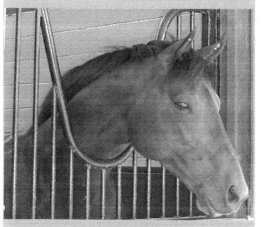

Rock of Gibraltar

Figure 6.4 Come Later might be the fastest horse on the track, but that is probably not where most people would place their bets. The smart money would go for the Rock of Gibraltar.

But if thought corrupts language, language can also corrupt thought.

George Orwell

if desired. It will not cause us to go to hell. Most people who teach that money is evil would gladly take someone else's money if it were given to them.

We should be careful of our definitions of money and wealth because this will greatly determine how we feel and act toward money. Our definition or labeling of something influences how we feel and act toward that thing. For example, would most people bet on a horse named "Come Later" or "Rock of Gibraltar?" "Come Later" might be the fastest horse on the track, but that is probably not where most people would place their bets. Therefore, people must be careful about the labels they accept as truthful about themselves and the world.

As stated earlier, if we find ourselves convinced that something is wrong or bad, we might avoid the thing — even if it is good for us. Some of us have also been taught that education takes us away from religion. There might be some truth in this statement. In his book *How We Believe: The Search for God in an Age of Science,* Michael Shemer refers to the correlation between education and religiosity. He states that as the educational level, especially scientific education, goes up, religiosity goes down.

Richard Dawkins also corroborates this notion in his book entitled *The God Delusion.* Dawkins cites a meta-analysis published by Paul Bell of the Mensa society in 2002. Bell looked at 43 studies conducted since 1927 on the relationship between religious belief and people's intelligence and/or educational level. Thirty-nine out of the forty-three studies found an inverse correlation. The higher a person's intelligence or education level, the less likely the person was religious.

The notion that education is wrong is the kind of thinking that appears to have thwarted scientific advancement in the Arab countries and helped to bring on the Dark Ages in Europe. This type of thinking fails to empower people. However, some so-called spiritual people have labeled education as a hindrance to being spiritual. Some courses such as philosophy and some theories in science, which teach us to ask questions and seek answers contrary to the teaching of our religion, we are told, we should avoid. Some of the scientific evidence, and theories such as evolution, could shatter our personal beliefs about God and creation.

We are told not to question our sacred books. The things that are not understood that make no sense to us should be accepted on faith. However, faith, which requires suspension of critical thinking, might not always equal truth with a high degree of certainty. It appears that we need to question our experts.

Neither the past nor the future exists. Between the past and the future, we find our lives in the present where choices have to be made. Even not making a choice is a choice.
Garland Sharp

As we would not choose a blueprint of a split foyer home to build a rancher, we should not choose disabling truths to build a successful life.
Garland Sharp

To different minds, the same world is a hell, and a heaven.
Emerson

Sometimes the experts promote certain truths to control the masses and sustain that control. This is not to suggest that everyone should abandon their religion — although in some cases, perhaps they should. If religion works positively for them, they might continue to be religious knowing that some truths are real, and others are perceived-real truths. These perceived real truths become effectively true because people believe them to be true. However, if their religion is disabling, they should take a critical look at their religion.

Again, we should be careful about the definitions or truths which we accept about ourselves and the world. Our definitions or perceived truths about ourselves and the world greatly determine our actions. For example, if a woman defined herself as fearful and defined the world as a scary, hostile place, she might live a life of fear and misery. In contrast, if she defined herself as fearless and defined the world as a place for opportunity, she might live a life of success and happiness.

Neither the past nor the future exists. Between the past and the future, we find our lives in the present where choices have to be made. Even not making a choice is a choice. For example, if we build a certain type of house, we need a blueprint for that specific house. If we build a different house, we need a different blueprint. As we must decide on the house desired and choose the right blueprint, we need to define ourselves and our world. Then, we need to choose the truth or blueprint to build our desired self and perceived world. As we would not choose a blueprint of a split foyer home to build a rancher, we should not choose disabling truths to build a successful life.

The choice is up to us about how we allow ourselves and our world to be defined. Even when it appears that we have no choices — such as in the harsh world of the Germans' concentration camps during World War II, there still are choices. Viktor Frankl in the book entitled *Man's Search for Meaning* states, "The concentration camp, as horrible as it was, could not take the last of human freedom." He describes the last of human freedom as "individuals being able to choose their attitude in any set of circumstances, to choose their own way." Although some men probably died in the camp, who chose to believe like Frankl, it would seem that they had a better chance of survival than those men who chose not to believe like Frankl. Some of the men who did not believe like Frankl simply gave up and died. Frankl lived to write about the horrors of the concentration camp. We have the power to choose. We have the power to define and redefine ourselves and our world. Many things might be taken from us, but there remains the power to choose our attitude in any situation. We have the power to choose our thoughts which, therefore, enable us to create better lives.

We can select more empowering definitions or truths about ourselves and our world. In this way, we avoid the destructive power of internal and external circumstances or "truth" created by ourselves and disabling external forces.

Figure 6.5 The concentration camp. As horrible as the camp was, it could not take the last of human freedom.

We who lived in concentration camps can remember the men who walked through the huts comforting others, giving away their last piece of bread. They may have been few in number, but they offer sufficient proof that everything can be taken from a man but one thing: the last of human freedom—to choose one's attitude in any given set of circumstances, to choose one's own way.

Viktor Frankl

Understand that the right to choose your own path is a sacred privilege. Use it. Dwell in possibility.
Oprah Winfrey

Chapter 7

Stratification – A Destructive Power of the Truth

If you live in India, England, America, or anywhere on Earth, you might find it hard to see the fallacy of your system when immersed in that system.
Garland Sharp

Class structures are a luxury that we cannot afford.

H. Rap Brown

Whether we are outcasts in India, poor whites in England, or blacks in America, to understand the power of hypnotic social beliefs, we might examine some ideologies and stratified systems which have affected and still affect billions of people. If we understand the fallacies of castes, classes, and racism, we might see those fallacies if they happen to exist, in our ideologies, systems and more importantly our self-limiting beliefs. Racism seems to be the most dangerous of the ideologies and systems for people all over the world. Therefore, this chapter spends more time debunking the ideology of racism. An ideology is a doctrine or belief that forms the basis for a particular system. It might be used to justify the social arrangement of the society. Therefore, we might consider any set of beliefs that justify a socially stratified system as an ideology.

Social stratification is a system used by a society to rank groups of people in a hierarchy. This system unequally stratifies people in that society. Two such socially stratified systems are class and caste. If individuals understand the development, preservation, and the effect that ideologies and stratified systems have on people, they might use this information to move toward better ways of thinking and better ways of being human.

If we understand the power of racism or the vast power of class and caste systems, we might be able to identify and eliminate our self-limiting beliefs. For example, if we can understand how and why a man accepts the definition of an outcast and lives his entire life as an outcast … and then passes this status on to future generations, we can see the tremendous power of socialization and social stratification. Once understood, whether we might be a black person in America, an impoverished person in England, or an outcast in India, we might be able to **de-hypnotize** ourselves and shed the negative effects of de-humanizing ideologies and systems.

We should not overlook the power of stratification. It appears that our status in the social hierarchy is extremely important — perhaps one of the most important things for us. Our status in the social hierarchy affects almost every facet of our lives. It affects such things as those whom we marry, what schools we attend, and the environment in which we are reared. These all affect our life chances. Therefore, the importance of understanding social stratification and its vast power over individuals in stratified systems is apparent.

Class, caste, and racist systems affect and have affected billions of people negatively. The ideologies that justify the social arrangements in these systems have become and remain part of the TFB-characteristics of people in these societies. Many people in these societies internalize and accept these ideologies, even when the result is their placement in the bottom stratum.

Class represents a form of stratification primarily based on economics or social status. In this system, individuals might move up or down in the system. Class systems exist in most societies. In some countries, class appears more apparent than in other countries. For example, some countries such as Saudi Arabia and Great Britain have a monarch. This type of ruler might have absolute power over the country, or might be a figurehead. The monarch's family is considered the royal family or royalty.

In a country such as England, people accidentally born in the upper class as royalty have greater access to social rewards than those accidentally born in the lower class as non-royalty. Because of their status in the social hierarchy, people considered royalty have many benefits that those considered non-royalty do not have. People considered royalty live in luxury while many people who believe them to be royalty live in poverty. Many of these poor people support and love the royal family. They support the system, and many are willing to die to maintain the system while remaining poor. They accept the system as being natural and right.

Although individuals might move up or down in a class system, many remain in the lower class. Even in America, there are large disparities throughout the system. The President of the United States lives in the White House. However, within walking distance of the White House, the author took the picture in Figure 7.2 on a cold January morning in Washington DC — a poor homeless soul sleeping under a blanket.

A caste system is another form of stratification that causes millions of people to have little access to social rewards, resulting from their status in the social hierarchy. One well-known caste is India's caste system. A caste system divides the society into strata determined by birth, and placement is usually permanent. Individuals do not choose their position in a caste system; their status in a caste system depends on the status of their parents. Unlike a class system, individuals do not usually move up or down in a caste system during their lifetime, if the system is sincerely believed and followed like the caste system in India.

Although India officially abolished the caste system in 1949, it still dominates the lives of millions of people, especially in rural India. The caste system has less influence in the urban areas where people are more educated and refined. We might find it hard to believe that it took until 1949 for the Indian government to officially abolish the caste system that had negatively affected the lives of billions of people for thousands of years. As in the *Planet of the Apes*, moving up in the caste system became the forbidden zone. This maintained stratification and gave some stability to the society.

Buckingham Palace – Home of Royalty

Figure 7.1 In England people accidentally born in the upper class as royalty have greater access to social rewards than those accidentally born in the lower class as non-royalty.

Figure 7.2 While the President lives in the White House, a few blocks away this poor homeless soul is sleeping outside under a blanket on a cold morning in January.

Figure 7.3 India's four castes (Not to scale). Below the Shudras or outside the Caste System we find the Harijans or the Outcasts.

Slaves are waiting for sale in Richmond, Virginia.

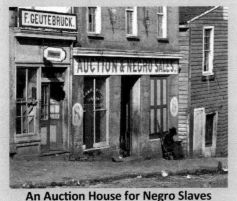

An Auction House for Negro Slaves
Figure 7.4 America's most infamous caste system was slavery. This system stratified millions of people.

India's caste system consists of four castes, with the highest being the Brahmans, which includes the priests and scholars. The next caste is the Kshatriyas, which includes the nobles and the warriors. Below the Kshatriyas are the Vaishyas, which includes the merchants and skilled artisans. The lowest caste is the Shudras, which includes common laborers. Below the Shudras or outside the caste system, one finds the Harijans — the Outcasts. These individuals make up the lowest of the society. The Shudras, as well as the Harijans, are frequently considered the untouchables for millions of people who live by the Caste System. The ones in the upper castes avoid touching, or in some cases even looking upon, the members of the lower castes.

In some ways, a caste system makes sense. It divides up labor. Not everyone can be a priest. Someone has to work. The fact that people accept their definition as outcasts, then live their entire lives in abject poverty and pass the status of outcasts on to future generations simply defies belief. This shows the power of stratification, however, and the tremendous power of belief on behavior.

America's most infamous caste system was slavery. This system stratified millions of people. After slavery, the Government passed segregation laws to aid in maintaining this stratification. Today, the continued racial discrimination against people causes some of them to have little access to social rewards, thereby helping to maintain stratification. Slavery, segregation, and discrimination are deeply ingrained within the ideology of racism.

A common definition of racism is, "the belief that one race is superior to another, which justifies the unequal treatment of the inferior race." However, this definition does not explain the fear that some whites appear to have of black people. Francis Cress Welsing's theory on racism might account for the fear that appears to be embedded in racism. She believed that whites developed the ideology of racism toward black people because of whites' inability to produce skin color, and the whites' fear of their race becoming extinct. Welsing states in her book entitled *"The Isis Papers, The Keys to Colors"* that, "Acutely aware of their inferior genetic ability to produce skin color, whites built the elaborate myth of white genetic superiority. Furthermore, whites set about the huge task of evolving a social, political, and economic structure that would support the myth of the inferiority of Blacks and other non-whites." Therefore, a better definition of racism might be "the belief that one racial group appears different from another and because of a false sense of superiority, feelings of inferiority, or feelings of fear, unequal treatment is justified." Such an ideology can cause people to be forced to inferior positions in society, where they have little access to social rewards. The racists try to justify their beliefs, to make the ideology of racism seem normal and right for people in the society.

Figure 7.5 A Black man drinking from a container marked "Colored" during segregation. After slavery, the government passed segregation laws to aid in maintaining stratification.

If you do not understand White Supremacy (Racism)—what it is, and how it works—everything else that you understand, will only confuse you.

Neely Fuller

Figure 7.6 All animals are equal, but some animals are more equal than others.
George Orwell (Animal Farm)

For example, in the past, individuals promoted the notion of Africans being subhuman. Therefore, they were suitable for slavery. Today the notion that blacks are inferior to whites still justifies many social and economic inequalities in America. The racist ideology tries to make the inequalities seem natural and right, causing people to accept a fallacious reality or myth presented to them.

Ashley Montague believed that the concept of race was a fallacious myth — 'our most dangerous myth.' He states in the book entitled, *Man's Most Dangerous Myth: The Fallacy of Race,* that "the idea of 'race' represents one of the greatest errors, if not the greatest error, of our time, and the most tragic." He further states, "Let us be human beings first and put the dangerous myth of 'race' in its proper place in the museum of ugly human errors."

Race is a myth, a dangerous myth; physiological differences identified as race are the results of the environmental adaptations of our ancestors. If we live or our ancestors lived in hot climates, our skin tends to be darker. If we live or our ancestors lived in cold climates, our skin tends to be lighter.

The color of our skin has nothing to do with us being inferior or superior. Whether we believe the story of Adam and Eve or the evolution of humans from lower biological forms, we would still conclude that all humans came from a common ancestry. The environment caused the mythical racial differences. There is but one race, the human race. Current scientific research leads to the conclusion that all humans originated from a common African ancestor.

The National Geographic Society, IBM, geneticist Spencer Wells, and the Waitt Family Foundation all corroborate this notion. They launched the Genographic Project, a five-year effort to understand the human journey and where humans came from and how they got to where they live today. This unprecedented task maps humanity's genetic journey throughout history. They state that "Fossil records fix human origins in Africa, but little is known about the great journey that took Homo Sapiens to the far reaches of the Earth." They conclude that all humans today descended from a common African ancestor who lived about 60,000 years ago. That Adam was not the only man living at the time, but the only man whose descendants survived until today.

With the overwhelming evidence that supports the origination of man in Africa and the over seven billon humans living today having a common ancestor, how did racism toward African and people of color in its modern form develop, and why? Research suggests that racism in its modern form developed simultaneously with European exploitation, conquest, and colonization of other countries. Theories of race began to develop to justify the Europeans' conquest and their unequal treatment of their colonized people. The racism of the

Figure 7.7 In the history of humankind, racism in its modern form is a recent development just as the computer, the electric light, the printing press, or any other recent development.

Europeans was on an international scale, supported by their religious and scientific communities.

Noam Chomsky further corroborates the notion that racism in its modern form is a recent development. He states, "There has always been racism. But it developed as a leading principle of thought and perception in the context of colonialism. That's understandable. When you have your boot on someone's neck, you have to justify it. The justification has to be their depravity. It's very striking to see this in the case of people who aren't very different from one another. Take a look at the British conquest of Ireland, the earliest of the Western colonial conquests. It was described in the same terms as the conquest of Africa. The Irish were a different race. They weren't human. They weren't like us. We had to crush and destroy them." The British defined the Irish as a different race. Although the Irish were white, the British defined them — as they did the black Africans — as non-humans. This justified the unequal treatment of the Irish.

Ashley Montague also corroborates the notion that racism in its modern form is a recent development. He states, "The 'racial' interpretation is a modern 'discovery.' That is the important point to grasp. The objection to any people on 'racial' or 'biological' grounds is virtually a modern innovation."

Audrey Smedley, an American social anthropologist, and Professor Emeritus at Virginia Commonwealth University in Anthropology and African-American studies, further corroborates this notion. He states, "Today's historians and social scientists in the Western World have reached the conclusion that the concept of race is a modern idea; it did not exist before the 17th Century and came to fruition gradually during the 18th Century." He further states, "The US race ideology, as a body of beliefs and attitudes about human differences, evolved in the wake of the establishment of slavery only for Africans and their descendants. The invention of race was primarily a product of efforts to justify slavery and the continuing conquest and exploitation of Native Americans..."

The fact that racism in its modern form is a **recent development** is one of the most profound notions in this book. In the history of humankind, racism in its modern form is a recent development just as the computer, the electric light, the printing press and many other recent developments. This myth has affected and still affects the lives of billions of people. This myth does not make **good nonsense**, let alone good sense. Although it has no scientific basis, it still determines how people are treated and their access to social rewards, to a significant degree.

Racism determines how individuals feel toward themselves and others. It determines how they see and treat themselves and others

The world's biggest problems today are really infinitesimal: the atom, the ovum, and a bit of pigment.
Herb Caen

What the world needs is not dogma but an attitude of scientific inquiry combined with a belief that the torture of millions is not desirable, whether inflicted by Stalin or by a Deity imagined in the likeness of the believer.
Bertrand Russell

as well as the way others see and treat them. Our status in the social hierarchy, based on race, clearly determines our access to social rewards in too many cases.

The revision of history further justified the myth of blacks' depravity and entrenched the Europeans' racist beliefs. The Europeans, writing of history, eliminated or removed many of the contributions of black people. Martin Bernal, in his book entitled *Black Athena,* argues that the Germans rewrote history after their defeat by Napoleon's armies at Jena in 1806. He states that the Germans saw the study of Greek history as a way to integrate people in a fragmented society. They developed the Aryan model of history, which is taught in much of the world today. Bernal states that "most people are surprised to learn that the Aryan Model, which most of us have been brought up to believe, developed only during the first half of the 19th century."

The Aryan model brought pride and integrated the German society while denying the Egyptians' significant contributions to history. This seems odd since the Germans had nothing to do with the Greek civilization.

Bernal states that Germans notable Karl Otfried Mullier replaced the Ancient Model of History with the Aryan Model. Bernal explains that according to the Ancient Model of History, the Greek culture had arisen because of colonization by black Egyptians and Phoenicians around 1500 B.C. We need to remember that the Egyptian civilization existed thousands of years before the Greek civilization existed. This fact has a high degree of plausibility based on historical records because the Egyptians wrote and drew pictures on wood and stone. This happened thousands of years before any known writing by the Greeks. According to Bernal, because of the racist thinking and an effort to integrate the German people to bring stability to the society, the German historians removed the contributions of the blacks to the Greek culture. This further supported the ideology of racism.

Ashley Montague believed racism to be the most dangerous myth. However, if racism is the most dangerous myth, the myth or ideology that supports caste systems has to be a very close second and the myth or ideology that supports class systems a close third. These false ideologies stratify societies and cause many people to suffer greatly. Racist, Caste, and Class systems make little or no sense. If we live in America, India, England, or anywhere else on earth, we might find it hard to see the fallacy of our system when immersed in that system. However, after examining this section on race, class, and caste, we might begin to see the fallacies in our systems and ideologies when dealing with race, class, castes, or any other self-limiting belief. Then, we might begin to redefine ourselves and our ideologies and systems.

Finally, a few words of caution might be in order. Although racism might be the most dangerous myth, all white people are not racist. Although class and caste systems might be built on dangerous myths, all people in the upper class and the upper caste are not evil.

Figure 7.8 Martin Bernal, in his books entitled *Black Athena*, argues that the Germans rewrote history and developed the Aryan model of history. He believed this model removed significant contributions of the Egyptians and Phoenicians from professed history.

Egyptian Coffin Panel with Paintings of Funerary Scenes   **Tutankhamun's burial mask**

Figure 7.9 We should remember that the Egyptian civilization existed thousands of years before Greece. This fact has a high degree of plausibility based on historical records because the Egyptians wrote and drew pictures on wood and stone. They also left artifacts of Pharaohs who had African features.

Although racism might be the most dangerous myth, all white people are not racist.

Garland Sharp

Chapter 8

Maintaining Stratification

Photo Caption

When we examine societies which have class, castes, and racist systems, we find that those at the top in these societies have advantages ... while those at the bottom suffer disadvantages, sometimes tragically. How could these forms of stratification be maintained in these societies for thousands of years? How could these forms of stratification keep billions of people powerless for so long? There must be some form of social control which causes people to accept their roles in these societies. If we examine the systems of social control in stratified systems, we might have a greater chance of finding ways to overcome the negative effects of class, castes, racism, or any other self-limiting systems or beliefs.

Robertson states that "Two factors, it seems, are vital in maintaining stratification: the ruling stratum control of the resources necessary to preserve the system and a general belief throughout the society that the inequality is actually 'natural' or 'right." In other words, the ruling stratum uses the big stick and the big lie to aid in maintaining stratification.

Social controls are exercised externally through such things as laws — the big stick — and internally by people's acceptance of the disabling TFB-characteristics of the society — the big lie. Certainly, it is the big lie that justifies or causes such things as castes, class, and racism to seem natural and right. These controls — whether externally or internally administered — help in maintaining the stratification of the society. The ruling stratum figuratively places chains on people's minds with the big lie and figuratively places chains on people's legs with the big stick.

Two additional factors appear vital in maintaining stratification. The third factor is that many people in the lower stratum spend most of their time and resources satisfying their basic survival needs. It appears that they have neither the time nor resources to work on social change. If they move beyond their basic survival needs, it appears that the fourth factor vital in maintaining stratification is that individuals fail to use what power and resources they have to end stratification. For them, good enough becomes good enough. Exhausted by their survival struggle, they acquiesce.

The first factor vital to maintaining stratification consists of the ruling stratum's control of the resources necessary to preserve the system. These people control or greatly influence the laws, wealth, power, the political system, information systems — and equally important — they control or influence the agents used to socialize people. Robertson states, "The laws in any society protect the rich, not the poor. The established religion supports the social order, rather than preaching its overthrow. Education teaches the virtues of the present system, not its vices. Government upholds the status quo, rather than undermining it." Robertson fails to mention that

Figure 8.1 The ruling stratum figuratively places chains on people's minds with the big lie and figuratively places chains on people's legs with the big stick.

the ruling stratum tries to control the information systems to support the social order instead of tearing the social order down. However, we are aware that internet sites such as Facebook and YouTube have aided in changing the social order. The internet aided in President Obama getting elected as the President of the United States of America and aided in tearing down the social order in Egypt under Hosni Mubarak. Certainly, Twitter aided Donald Trump in becoming President of the United States.

Governments develop and pass laws to preserve the system. In many ways, these laws protect the rich — not the poor. For example, Congress passes laws that favor the rich and large corporations. Past segregation laws have caused discrimination for many American blacks. They could not attend certain schools or live in certain neighborhoods.

Because of slavery, segregation, discrimination, and laws favoring the wealthy, many blacks do not have the wealth to transfer to their kids as do many whites. Therefore, many black kids start at an economic disadvantage compared with whites. Jesse Jackson compares a poor black person with a rich white person — both born in America. He compares the poor black person to a batter at home plate, and the rich white person to a player starting out at third base. Many people start at a disadvantage because the laws aid some and hinder others, thus maintaining stratification.

Figure 8.2 The Capitol Building. Governments develop and pass laws to preserve the system.

Landholders ought to have a share in the government to support these invaluable interests and check the other many. They ought to be so constituted as to protect the minority of the opulent against the majority.
James Madison

The United States is a nation of laws: badly written and randomly enforced.
Frank Zappa

Figure 8.3 Richard Dawkins states that when he lived in America in the late 1960s, 'law and order' was a politician's code for anti-black prejudice.

As stated earlier, the established religion supports the social order, rather than advocating its overthrow. The Hindu religion supports the caste system in parts of India. In these areas, the Hindu religion teaches that the individual's status in the next life is based on their conformity to the required behavior of their present caste. Based on their behavior, they might be reincarnated to a higher caste, lower caste, or as an animal. This causes people to predictably support the social order. This belief serves the interests of the people in the upper stratum while causing people in the lower stratum to suffer greatly.

Figure 8.4 US Congressional Buildings – "In God We Trust" Plaque.

The kingdom of heaven is within.

Jesus

You make your own heaven or hell right here on Earth.

The Temptations

The powers that be are ordained by God.

The Bible

Figure 8.5 Spirit of the Frontier by John Gast. Gast painted a popular scene of people moving west that captured the view of Americans at the time they believed in Manifest Destiny.

Christianity has supported and still supports the social order in America. Christianity supported the American slavery system. In the Bible, it states that Apostle Paul said, "Slaves obey your masters." This was taken literally to support slavery. The idea that God cursed the biblical Ham and turned him black for laughing at Noah while Noah was drunk and naked supported the notion that Africans were suitable for slavery. Also, the doctrine of Christianity declares that when people die, they will go to heaven or hell. Many people accept this belief and spend most of their time focusing on getting to heaven. In the Bible, Lazarus, the poor man, appears to be the hero and the rich man appears to be the antihero. Lazarus dies and goes to Abraham's bosom, and the rich man dies and goes to hell. Many people spend their time focusing and working for a mansion in the sky, and avoiding hell while forgetting to work on social changes. They become content at the bottom of the socioeconomic ladder, thus aiding in preserving the system.

Christian preachers have taught that every man is subject to a higher power. This supports the social order. On television, the pastor of one of the largest Christian churches in the world stated that people should obey their bosses or any other person in power because God put these people in power. He stated that individuals should obey the ones in power even if the individuals find the people in power to be evil. He quoted the Bible in Romans 13, "That the ones in power are ordained by God. Whosoever resists the power resists the ordinances of God. They that resist shall receive damnation."

This type of thinking and other similar beliefs supports and have supported the social order. Other past beliefs that supported the social order were the notion of the divine rights of kings in the Feudal system of Medieval Europe and Manifest Destiny during the settlement of the western United States. In Medieval Europe, individuals believed that for generation after generation, God put the Kings in power. During the early American western settlement, settlers believed in Manifest Destiny. They believed that it was their destiny to own the land in the western parts of the United States. Although the divine rights of kings and Manifest Destiny might seem far-fetched to the average individual living today, many still hold on to similar thinking such as God ordaining evil leaders and gods being on their side in wars.

Education supports the social order by teaching the virtues of the society, not the vices. As stated earlier, one purpose of the educational system is to socialize individuals with the existing TFB-characteristics of the society. People usually conform to the existing TFB-characteristics of the society, even when in the lower stratum.

Figure 8.6 Ancient or pre-Islamic Egyptians. These were people of color. They existed long before there was ever a Greece. The Ancient pre-Islamic Egyptians were black Africans. We see here, as in many of the Egyptian artifacts, that the nose of the figurine is broken, some believe, to hide the African features.

Who controls the past controls the future. Who controls the present controls the past.

George Orwell

History is a weapon.

Anonymous

It appears many blacks, outcasts, and poor whites find themselves socialized to feel inferior to those in the upper stratum and conform to this idea of inferiority. Education aids in preserving the system. For example, we find very little black history in the American school system. When we examine many of the history books in schools, we might conclude that black people made few or no significant contributions to history. The ruling stratum controls what the schools teach about history. The versions of history taught in America's schools aid in maintaining the current social arrangement. It comes as no surprise that we cannot find the Ancient Model of History which many believe was destroyed by the Europeans, taught in most American schools.

If Bernal was right, we could see the importance of this history, if we examine the primary reason which Bernal maintained that the Europeans destroyed the Ancient Model of History and created the Aryan Model. The European leaders tried to bring stability and pride to a fragmented society. The leaders correctly recognized that individuals knowing the positive aspects of their history aid in building pride and high self-esteem.

Many American blacks who have gone through the American school system can only trace their history as far back as slavery. Many blacks believe the story of a white Adam and Eve. Believing this supplants the more realistic view that man originated in Africa. Myths like the Piltdown man — a cave man, discovered in England and later identified as a hoax — and the Aryan Model have been used to distort history. Many blacks as well as whites have no idea or refuse to believe that the Ancient or pre-Islamic Egyptians were people of color. They existed long before there was a Greece. The Ancient pre-Islamic Egyptians appear to have been black Africans.

Government supports the social order of the society, rather than undermining it. If individuals try to eliminate the social order or become equal with the upper class, this might be regarded as a threat to the society. For example, blacks trying to achieve equal rights in the South in the sixties threatened the social order. The American government tried to crush the dissenters in the South as long as possible. Governments pass laws to keep the dissenters under control. If laws fail to work, the ruling stratum might imprison or kill the dissenters. For example, non-conformists or dissenters such as Malcolm X, Martin Luther King, Galileo, Bruno, and Mandela lost their lives or became incarcerated. Laws have kept many people trapped at the bottom of stratified systems. The ruling stratum uses laws, religion, schools, government, and whatever means necessary to maintain the social order.

The second factor vital to maintaining stratification is a general belief throughout the society that the inequality is natural and right.

Figure 8.7 Adolf Hitler. One of the most infamous leaders in all of history has been purported to have said, "What luck for rulers that men do not think."

Grandmother

The author as a boy   The Author

Figure 8.8 Although intellectually the belief that wearing a cap or hat in the house will cause bad luck had a low probability of being true, this belief shaped behaviors by the author long after his grandmother died.

As stated earlier, an ideology is a body of beliefs that establishes the basis for a system. The dominant ideology of a society favors the upper class. This ideology justifies the ruling upper class being on top and the lower class being on the bottom. The ruling stratum establishes and seeks to maintain the ideology to justify the social arrangement. Individuals throughout the society have to accept — or at least conform to — this arrangement, if the stratification is to survive. Some people might move up in the system, but if the system is to survive intact, the majority of the people in the system must accept and remain in their status, thinking that the status is natural and right.

Robertson profoundly states, "Most social control, however, does not have to be exercised through the direct influence of other people. We exercise it ourselves, internally. Growing up in society involves the internalization of norms — the unconscious process of making conformity to norms of one's culture part of one's personality, so that one usually follows social expectations automatically, without question." Carter Woodson corroborates this notion. He states, "If you can control a man's thinking, you don't have to worry about his actions. If you can determine what a man thinks, you do not have to worry about what he will do."

The socialization agents socialize individuals from birth to death to consciously and unconsciously accept the norms of the culture, which include the prevailing ideology. It appears that Robertson was right. People make conformity to the norms of the culture part of their personality. Then, they exercise the norms internally without much direct influence from other people. These people find themselves "internally controlled." This notion is not new.

To illustrate, one of your author's grandmothers instilled in her grandchildren internal controls to cause them to adopt certain norms and prevent them from having certain behaviors. For example, if a male wore a cap or hat indoors, this grandmother became upset. She believed that males wearing a cap or hat indoors would cause bad luck. She instilled this belief in her grandsons. The internalization of this belief made the author feel uncomfortable wearing a cap or hat indoors. Although intellectually this belief had a low probability of being true, this belief shaped behaviors by the author long after his grandmother died.

After we accept and internalize our thinking, feeling, and behaving characteristics for a period of time, these characteristics become ingrained. It appears difficult for us to change our behavior, even if there is no direct influence from other people. Religion clearly illustrates this notion. Religion makes individuals predictable and aids in social control. People strive to please their gods, to avoid such things as returning to life in a lower caste or being sent to hell.

After we accept the TFB-characteristics for a period of time, such as Grandmother conditioning me that wearing a hat indoors brought bad luck, it appears difficult to change behavior even if there is no physical punishment. It was difficult for me to wear a hat in the house long after Grandmother died.

Garland Sharp

If you can control a man's thinking, you don't have to worry about his actions. If you can determine what a man thinks, you do not have to worry about what he will do. If you can make a man believe that he is inferior, you don't have to compel him to seek an inferior status; he will do so without being told, and if you can make a man believe that he is justly an outcast, you don't have to order him to the back door, he will go to the back door on his own and if there is no back door, the very nature of the man will demand that you build one.

Carter G. Woodson

Believing notions such as conforming outcasts being reincarnated in a higher caste and rich people being sent to hell, people accept being poor and powerless to the will of gods. This supports the general belief throughout the society that these artificial inequalities are 'natural' or 'right.'

People develop comfort zones and act out the role of being poor or outcasts without much influence from other people. They feel uncomfortable when they move out of their comfort zones. As with the belief by the author about wearing a hat indoors, people might find it hard to shed internalized beliefs even when they consciously reject these beliefs.

People might remain poor, even when they consciously cease believing that it is God's will for them to be poor. Subconsciously, the belief might still control their actions. As Freud stated, "the subconscious mind without being known by the individual causes them to behave irrationally." People sometimes consciously and unconsciously accept irrational beliefs and behave irrationally as outcasts, the fourth generation of unwed mothers, or people who have bad luck because they wear hats indoors.

Individuals consciously and unconsciously follow the social expectations of the society, thus aiding in preserving the system. As Carter Woodson states, "If you can control a man's thinking, you don't have to worry about his actions." As we know, our conscious and unconscious process of making conformity to norms or expectations of the culture part of our personality, causes us to follow social expectations without much external control. As individuals in the lower stratum internalize the TFB-characteristics of the society, they come to believe that the social arrangement is natural or right. They have what Karl Marx called false consciousness.

False consciousness is an ideology accepted by individuals that keeps them from seeing the true nature of their plight, which justifies their social arrangement in a system. For example, outcasts in India might believe that their status is based on deeds done in a previous life. Poor black people in America might believe their status in life is based on the will of God. Both groups look for something outside of themselves and their oppressors as the cause of their plight. They blame deeds of a previous life, God, or some other thing that they are unable to control as the cause of their plight.

This false consciousness aids the ruling stratum in maintaining social control because people in the bottom stratum accept the false consciousness. They remain at the bottom believing that something beyond them and their oppressors caused their plight. They fail to move from false consciousness to class consciousness. Class consciousness is an ideology accepted by individuals which causes them to see the true nature of their plight as an oppressed group and to question their social arrangement in the system.

Because of the ruling stratum's control of the resources and the general belief throughout the society that artificial inequalities are natural or right, many people find great difficulty moving from false consciousness to class consciousness, thus preserving the system. Because of internal and external controls, they find difficulty in being dissenters in a system that rewards conformists and punishes dissenters. Thus conforming, they fail to move to class consciousness.

The third factor that aids in preserving the system is that many individuals in the lower stratum spend most of their time and resources satisfying their basic survival needs. If we look at Maslow's hierarchy of needs — physiological, security, social, esteem, and self-actualization —, many people spend most of their time satisfying the lower needs. They never reach the higher needs such as esteem and self-actualization. They fail to reach their full potential. Therefore, many people find themselves trapped in their system even when they move from false consciousness to class consciousness, and recognize the fallacy of the system. They still spend most of their time and energy trying to survive and to obtain some of the resources controlled by the ruling stratum.

All men are not created equally. Some have more talent, intelligence, and wealth than others. Someone born in rural India as a mentally-challenged outcast is not created equal to someone born

Karl Marx

Figure 8.9 According to Karl Marx, people who suffer from false consciousness, instead of blaming the system, attribute their low status to something beyond their control.

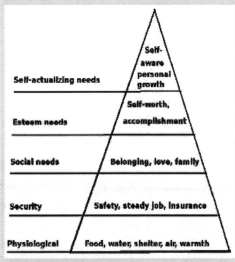

Figure 8.10 Maslow's Hierarchy of Needs.

Figure 8.11 Outcasts in India. Some people are more equal than others. A common quote used by many people. These outcasts are certainly less equal than those in the higher castes.

Some people are born on third base and go through life thinking they hit a triple.

Barry Switzer

Success is to be measured not so much by the position that one has reached in life as by the obstacles which he has overcome.
Booker T. Washington

in England as royalty with wealth and high intelligence. The intelligent person born in England inherits a hereditary blueprint and environment superior to the hereditary blueprint and environment of the mentally challenged outcast born in rural India. The person born in England as royalty might one day be the Prince or Queen of England, but the mentally challenged outcast living in rural India would probably remain an outcast. Even if they had similar talents and intelligence at birth, the person in England has a much better chance of living a successful life than the outcast born in India. This example might seem extreme, but such people do indeed exist.

Some make the argument that everyone has the same amount of time in the day, thereby arguing equality. However, the poor might spend most of their time trying to acquire the things the wealthy already have. The wealthy might spend most of their time creating, learning, and growing while the poor might spend most their time fighting to survive. It could be compared to running a 100-meter race, where the wealthy person starts out 50 meters ahead of the poor person. If people busy themselves getting the necessities, they might not have the time or inclination to create, learn, and grow. They might have little time to work on social change. Instead of creating, learning, and growing, many people in the lower stratum spend most of their time trying, sometimes without success, to satisfy their basic needs. As stated earlier, many people in the lower stratum spend most of their time and resources satisfying their basic survival needs. This is vital to maintaining stratification.

The fourth factor vital to maintaining stratification and preserving the system is that people fail to use the power and resources they have, to change the system. If they move beyond fulfilling their survival needs, they still conform to the existing ideology without much external control. This is partly due to the second factor that is vital to maintaining stratification, the general belief throughout the society that the inequality is natural or right. For example, many times in America as blacks move up the ladder of success and move to the suburbs, they fail to see or acknowledge the plight of others. They spend their extra time and money on events that do nothing to bring about social change. Many of them are more concerned about whether their favorite sports team won today than how many people died in the war in the Middle East or died of AIDS in Africa, today. Many of these people fail to organize to bring about social change, and thus the stratified system persists.

It is not easy for men to rise whose qualities are thwarted by poverty.
Juvenal

Figure 8.13 Success. Many people obtain success thus enabling them to organize for social change.

Figure 8.12 This lady appears to have time but lacks the resources for success.

What material success does is provide you with the ability to concentrate on other things that really matter. That is being able to make a difference, not only in your own life, but also in other people's lives.
Oprah Winfrey

It seems that because people consciously and unconsciously conform to the existing ideology without much external control, that if all the power and resources were evenly distributed, in a few years the power and resources could be back in the hands of the existing ruling stratum. Therefore, it appears that to control individuals, in many cases, the ruling stratum need not place chains on individuals' legs using the big stick; they need only place chains on individuals' minds through social controls, using the big lie. However, if the big lie does not cause individuals to conform, the ruling stratum might put chains on the individuals' legs using the big stick.

It appears to control people; in many cases, the ruling stratum need not place chains on individuals' legs using the big stick, they need only place chains on individuals' minds, using the big lie. However, if the big lie does not cause individuals to conform, the ruling stratum might put chains on the individuals' legs using the big stick.

Garland Sharp

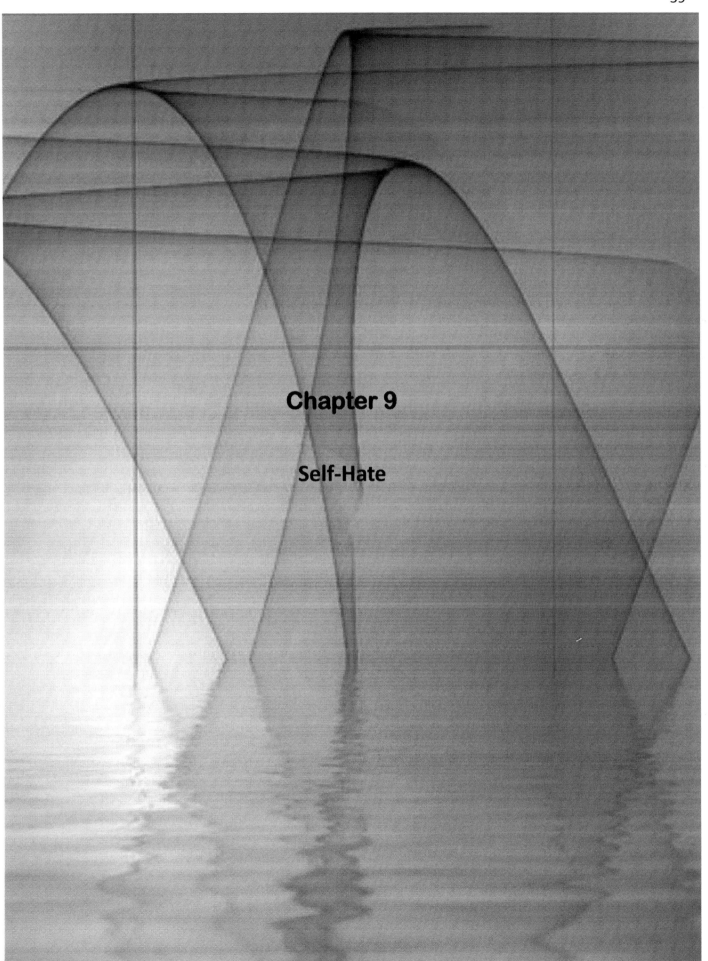

Chapter 9

Self-Hate

It is easier to build strong children than to repair broken men.
Frederick Douglass

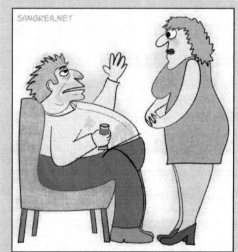

Figure 9.1 Individuals should be independent of the good opinion of others.

The "self-image" is the key to human personality and human behavior. Change the self-image and you change the personality and the behavior.
Maxwell Maltz

As stated in chapter eight, the ruling stratum usually does not need to place chains on people's legs using the big stick; they only need to place chains on people's minds using the big lie. One of the biggest lies centers on the notion of self-hate. Christian states, "If the environment in which we are nurtured inhibits the development of an integrated self and/or instills negative feeling about that self — self-hate in its many forms — then the quality of our existence can be permanently damaged."

Dr. Belinda Trotter, who taught at the University of Tennessee, corroborates this notion. She argues that "If a demented care-giver nurtured a child and treated the child as the opposite sex until around age three, the effects on the child would be irreversible." The child, even if he is a boy, internalizes the feelings of being a girl. The boy might look in the mirror unclothed and intellectually know that he is a boy, but would always view himself and feel like a girl. We can clearly see that in extreme cases, circumstances can inhibit the development of an integrated self, and the quality of our existence can be permanently damaged.

Christian states, "What each of us can become during our lifetime is determined by two fundamental conditions: (1) the degree to which we experience a more or less consistent self or identity, and (2) whether the feelings we developed about that self are predominantly good." As stated earlier, the self is individuals' distinct way of being human based on their unique TFB-characteristics. The self is the conscious being who experiences the world.

We should develop and experience a consistent self, independent of the good opinion of others. Although Christian believes that what we can become is determined by the degree to which we experience a consistent self, this probably does not mean that the self cannot or should not be improved. In many cases, change might be necessary. We might need to change the self and view ourselves in more empowering ways, for example.

As noted earlier, the self-image is the way we view ourselves. This view of self may or may not be accurate, with high probability. For example, a woman might view herself as being overweight, when most of her friends and her physician consider her to be dangerously underweight. We each develop feelings about our self-image. These feelings about the self or the feelings about our self-image might simply be considered self-esteem. Self-esteem could be defined as how we feel about ourselves, or how much we like ourselves. Our self-image might be false or have a low probability of being true, but our self-esteem is just the way we feel. We could say that our self-esteem is always true or has a high probability of being true. But assuredly, high self-esteem is the opposite of self-hate.

In a Masters' Degree thesis prepared by the author while attending the University of Tennessee, the research and data analysis showed a positive correlation among self-efficacy, self-esteem, and success in the classroom. The students in training classes measured as having the higher self-esteem and self-efficacy made higher grades on written tests. This corroborates the notion that what individuals can become and achieve is partly determined by how they view and feel about themselves. This is good and bad news.

Most people do not have to deal with problems as difficult as being nurtured as the opposite sex, as described by Dr. Belinda Trotter. However, many people, especially those in the lower stratum, have inner problems resulting from self-hate. These inner problems and self-hate come about because the environment inhibits the development of an integrated self and/or instills negative feelings about the self in the form of low self-esteem, a negative self-image, and other self-limiting beliefs and feelings.

Self-hate makes people feel unworthy to have the good things in life. Unworthiness is one of the chief reasons they remain trapped in negative situations. Self-hate negatively affects people regardless of whether the person is a black in America, a poor white in England, or an outcast in India. This self-hate perpetuates false consciousness and aids in maintaining stratification ... making their plight in the lower class seem natural and right.

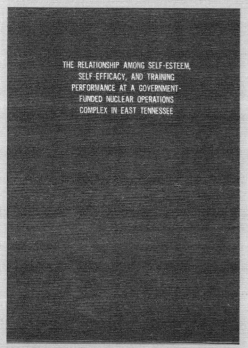

THE RELATIONSHIP AMONG SELF-ESTEEM, SELF-EFFICACY, AND TRAINING PERFORMANCE AT A GOVERNMENT-FUNDED NUCLEAR OPERATIONS COMPLEX IN EAST TENNESSEE

Figure 9.3 Sharp's Master Thesis. This document is on file at the University of Tennessee in Knoxville, Tennessee. Your author found that the higher the individuals' self-esteem and self-efficacy, the higher they scored on written tests.

Figure 9.2 English: Sad female head by Ernst Ludwig Kirchner. The feelings of self-hate can cause individuals to be extremely sad.

> Low self-esteem is like driving through life with your hand-brake on.
> **Maxwell Maltz**

> Of all the traps and pitfalls in life, self-disesteem is the deadliest, and the hardest to overcome, for it is a pit designed and dug by our own hands summed up in the phrase, "It's no use—I can't do it."
> **Maxwell Maltz**

How we see ourselves, how we see each other should be determined by us, not by people who generally don't like us: people who pass laws certifying us as less human. We're going to have to decide for ourselves what we are and what we're not. Create our own image of ourselves. And nurture it and feed it till it stands on its own.

Sidney Poitier

You will act like the sort of person you conceive yourself to be. Not only this, but you literally cannot act otherwise, in spite of all your conscious effort or will power. The man who conceives himself as a failure-type person will find some way to fail...

Maxwell Maltz

If the ruling stratum can persuade or get the lower class socialized to host self-hate in any of its many forms, the ruling stratum could keep these people at the bottom of the socioeconomic ladder for generation after generation. This appears to have happened in America with some blacks, in England with some people considered non-royalty, and in India with outcasts. It seems that these people were socialized to view themselves as inferior to others, and to harbor feelings of self-hate. This limits what they will attempt and what they will accomplish. These feelings of self-hate aid in determining their comfort zone. This self-hate limits what they feel worthy of having or becoming, stunting their mental growth and achievement.

If a man fails to view himself in a particular role, such as being wealthy, he probably will not seek wealth. If he does try, he might give only a half-hearted effort. If people do succeed at something beyond their comfort zone, they sometimes unconsciously or consciously move back down to the place where they feel they belong. For example, if a man views himself as a poor person and has feelings of self-hate, he might feel unworthy of having plenty of money. If he receives a lot of money, he would probably find ways to rid himself of the money. This might explain what happens to some people who win the lottery. They move back to their comfort zone or where they feel they belong by ridding themselves of the lottery money through ill-advised actions.

If we look around, we might see other examples of people moving back into their comfort zone. For example, in Humboldt, Tennessee, your author's hometown, there was an impoverished family with about ten children. They lived in an old, ragged house. To help them, people from the City's Housing Development authorized building the family a new house. In a few months after the family moved into the new house, the new house began to look like the old house. After about a year, the family had almost destroyed the house. Destroying the house put them back in their comfort zone or the familiar conditions of living in a ragged, dilapidated house.

The same appears to hold true for three and four generations of unwed mothers. They exhibit self-hate in its many forms. They view themselves as unwed mothers, and becoming unwed mothers and living in poverty are part of their comfort zone. Many impoverished unwed mothers, destitute non-royalty, underprivileged blacks, and outcasts appear to exhibit self-hate in its many forms and become comfortable in their comfort zones.

What if people started treating these people differently? What if people suddenly started treating a man considered an outcast as upper caste and moved him to an environment of luxury? This would probably make him very uncomfortable. The outcast would be out of his comfort zone. He would probably try to move back to conditions where he felt comfortable. This appears to be one of the main reasons people remain in poverty or remain outcasts. They become victims of false consciousness and remain in their comfort zones without much direct influence from other people. These people in the lower stratum have internalized their diminished status. When they act otherwise, stress causes them to feel uncomfortable. Many times they will do something to get back to the place where they believe they belong, back in their comfort zone. They become voluntary prisoners. They become institutionalized.

Self-hate — in the form of a negative self-image, low self-esteem, and feelings of unworthiness — can damage the quality of our existence. This negative self-hate, together with the notion that we will do better in the after-life as a result, contribute to countless people remaining victims of false consciousness. We remain content with our stations in life. For example, many blacks and poor whites in America have feelings of self-hate. This, coupled with the notion that one day they will go to heaven where the streets are paved with gold, aid in making them content with their stations in life. Feelings of self-hate plus the notion of reincarnation to a higher status aid in making many outcasts content with their stations in life. The notion of individuals going to heaven or being reincarnated to a higher status, coupled with feelings of self-hate, produce the same results. Both cause individuals to accept the reality presented to them and remain in the lower stratum ... as victims of false self-consciousness. As individuals in the lower stratum look for better futures after death, they become less powerful and poorer while the individuals in the upper stratum become more powerful and wealthier.

The ruling stratum — in many cases — can control the environment and influence the socializing agents to inhibit our development of an integrated self, thereby instilling self-hate in us. As stated said earlier, this can permanently damage the quality of our lives. In a case like the boy raised as the opposite sex until age three, to overcome this damage, this process could be long and agonizing. However, experiencing a consistent self which we feel predominately good about, removing self-hate in its many forms, makes embarking on the process seem worth the effort. We all should strive to remove self-hate in its many forms, replacing it with self-love. We need self-love in forms such as high self-esteem, positive self-images, high self-worth, and other empowering beliefs and feelings. With self-love, we can live more empowering lives. We should shed the negative truth that renders us unworthy, and realize that we are as worthy to have the finer things in life as anyone else. We should develop a better truth and rise above stratification if we find ourselves in the lower stratum.

In every aspect of our lives, we are always asking ourselves, how am I of value? What is my worth? Yet, I believe that worthiness is our birthright.
Oprah Winfrey

PART THREE

DEVELOPING A BETTER TRUTH

Chapter 10

Worthiness - Rising Above Stratification

You take the blue pill — the story ends; you wake up in your bed and believe whatever you want to believe. You take the red pill — you stay in Wonderland, and I show you how deep the rabbit-hole goes.

Morpheus in the Matrix

We know that individuals can be acculturated into any set of customs, beliefs, and values; they can be made to believe, value and even worship almost anything. If societies can condition us, then we know that we can be unconditioned and reconditioned.
James Christian

By gaining Class Consciousness and seeing the true nature of their plight as an oppressed group in the social arrangement, will the downtrodden stop believing the existing ideologies and begin to develop new ideologies? People must question the existing truths and develop new truths. They must recognize the enormous power of ideologies or truths that cause them to accept inferior statuses such as being outcasts in India, non-royalty in England, or poor blacks/whites in America and passing this status on to future generations.

People in the lower stratum must recognize that the real cause of their plight is mostly humans, which includes themselves — not God, luck, or fate. They must accept that it is people who developed systems and ideologies such as castes, class, and racism, not God. There was no such thing as castes, class, or racist systems until people developed and others accepted these irrational and evil systems. We should all, especially those in the lower stratum, shed the beliefs of these negative systems.

This leads us back to the notion of worthiness. Individuals must realize that they are just as worthy of the good things in life as others — in the upper stratum. As stated earlier, unworthiness appears to be one of the chief reasons people remain trapped in negative situations. Therefore, people in the lower stratum must define themselves equally as worthy as the people in the upper stratum. We know that, if we do not feel worthy of a thing, we might not try to attain that thing. If we receive or accomplish the thing, we might then do something to get back to our comfort zone. Our feelings of worthiness strongly influence the comfort zone. Our comfort zone can aid in keeping us in the lower stratum.

Figure 10.1 Individuals must gain Class Consciousness and see the true nature of their plight as an oppressed group and question their social arrangement in the system.

Queen Victoria

Close stool (Commode)

Figure 10.2 Even the queen had to eliminate waste.

We should learn to redefine ourselves and declare that we are as worthy as anyone. No person is better than another person. If you take the time to read, understand, and believe the next few sentences, it can help to eliminate stratification, shed false consciousness, eliminate other self-limiting beliefs, and move you toward class consciousness and empowerment. "There is but one class, first class. There is but one caste, upper caste. There is but one race, the human race. The only person better than **"You"** is the person who does not doo-doo." Hopefully, the use of the foul language and the first person **"You"** emphasize the point.

No group of people is better or more worthy than another group — no royalty, no upper caste, and no superior races. That is all foolishness. We need to believe that there is but one class, first class. There is but one caste, upper caste. There is but one race, the human race. No matter how good individuals look, no matter how much they snub their noses at others, and no matter how much they try to make others feel inferior, they still have to pull up their pretty dresses or pull down their pants and sit on the commode, squat toilet, or whatever the h... they use and eliminate waste.

Each person, whether non-royalty in England, an outcast in India, or poor black in America, is as worthy as the Queen of England, the Priest in India, or the President of the United States. The Queen, the Priest, and the President all eliminate waste. Therefore, they are no better than anyone else.

We must realize that no mythical class is better than another mythical class. No mythical caste is better than another mythical caste. No mythical race is better than another mythical race. Although the Queen of England appears to have the more important position, she is no better than the well-meaning school teacher in England. The Brahman priests and scholars appear to have the more important positions. Yet, they are no better than the outcast who washes the laundry. The white chief executive officer running a major corporation in America appears to have the more important position. He is no better than the well-meaning black worker running the machinery on the factory floor.

No matter how good individuals look, no matter how much they snub their noses at others, and no matter how much they try to make others feel inferior, they still have to pull up their pretty dresses or pull down their pants and sit on the commode, squat toilet, or whatever the h... they use and eliminate waste.

Garland Sharp

There is but one class, first class. There is but one caste, upper caste. There is but one race, the human race. The only person better than **"You"** is the person who does not doo-doo.

Garland Sharp

Photo Caption

Is it not written in your laws that I said that ye are gods?
Jesus

It is no measure of health to be well adjusted to a profoundly sick society.

Jiddu Krishnamurti

If your happiness depends on what somebody else does, I guess you do have a problem.
Richard Bach

Figure 10.3 Slave Children. There is no such thing as a well-adjusted slave.

If we can choose to work toward our desires, we should adopt the truth that no person is better than another person ... based on such nonsense as class, caste, race, or for that matter "God's chosen people." We should view ourselves as worthy as any other person to have the things that we desire. If unsuccessful, and we choose to live successfully, we must redefine ourselves and adopt a set of beliefs or ideology which empowers us.

We should develop new ideologies which support a self with high self-esteem, a positive self-image, and feelings of worthiness. If the outcasts had a positive sense of self with high self-esteem, a realistic self-image, and feelings of worthiness ... they would not accept their definition as outcasts. They would not accept the harsh reality presented to them. They would realize that their status results from them being accidentally born to parents in the lower stratum.

This lower stratum was developed and defined by humans, not gods. If born to parents of the upper caste, they would be defined differently. If someone switched an outcast position at birth with a person in the upper caste, the outcast would be in the upper caste and the other person would be the outcast. Their lives would be totally different — based on their caste.

Those of us who suffer from false consciousness should rid ourselves of socialized self-limiting beliefs. We must not accept these self-limiting beliefs, conform to our roles, nor live with feelings of unworthiness. It does not matter if we are a black person in the United States, a poor white person in England, or an outcast in India, we should change and shed the feelings of unworthiness. We might need to divest ourselves of the TFB-characteristics that support our ideology or system. For example, if a woman is an impoverished person in England or America, she might need to become decaucasianized from the beliefs that support classism and racism developed by Caucasians. If she lives in India, she might need to become dearyanianized from the beliefs that support caste systems developed by Aryans.

People must realize that each person is inherently as good as any other human being and deserves success and happiness as much as any other person. Whether they deserve success and happiness should not be based on their skin color, class, or caste, but as Dr. King said, by the content of their character. Therefore, we should evaluate our truths and see the true nature of our plight as an oppressed group ... and question our social arrangement in the system. We might need to develop new ideologies. We must recognize that the main cause of our plight is not a god, fate, or luck. Our plight is caused primarily by humans. Our plight is caused by us as individuals, and others who have their feet on our neck.

Chapter 11

Evaluating the Truth

I was gratified to be able to answer promptly. I said, I don't know.
Mark Twain

Figure 11.1 The Thinker by Rodin. Individuals should take the time to think. If critically evaluated, many of the truths and ideologies they have accepted might be discarded.

For centuries, theologians have been explaining the unknowable in terms of the-not-worth-knowing.
H. L. Mencken

If we want to move from false consciousness to class consciousness and from self-hate to self-love, we should critically evaluate the truths and ideologies we accept and have accepted into our lives. We should critically evaluate our worldview, which includes how we view ourselves. If critically evaluated, many of the truths and ideologies which we have accepted might be discarded. For example, your author discarded many TFB-characteristics from his worldview concerning racism after a critical evaluation. Many of the same TFB-characteristics — if we fail to toss them out —influence our worldview and cripple our thinking.

Critical thinking starts when we stop accepting and start critically evaluating the many opinions accepted as true. Brooke Moore and Richard Parker, in the book entitled, *Critical Thinking,* define critical thinking as "the careful, deliberate determination of whether we should accept, reject, or suspend judgment about a claim — and the degree of confidence with which we accept or reject the claim."

Myers, in the book entitled *Psychology,* argues that critical thinking is "thinking that does not blindly accept arguments and conclusions. Rather, it examines assumptions, discerns hidden values, evaluates evidence, and assesses conclusions." He believes that when using critical thinking before accepting an idea or belief from others, a person might ask the following questions: "How do they know that? What is this person's agenda? Is the conclusion based on anecdote and gut feeling, or on evidence? Does the evidence justify a cause-effect conclusion? What alternative explanations are possible?"

Some folks do an awful lot of talking without brains.
Dorothy in the Wizard of OZ

I owe my success to having listened respectfully to the very best advice, and then going away and doing the exact opposite.
G. K. Chesterton

If anyone critically evaluated a worldview that supported class, caste, and racist systems — applying Moore and Parker's definition of critical thinking and using Myers' questions for critical thinking — then many ideas, beliefs, values, and thinking habits would probably be immediately discarded. If enough people critically evaluated such notions as racism in America, the Caste System in rural India, and royalty in England; these would cease to exist on a wide scale.

How do we become better critical thinkers and recognize "truths" that correspond closer to real world objects/events? As discussed earlier, our truth is only a representation of real world objects/events. Therefore, it is extremely difficult to be absolutely sure — or 100% sure — of any information. We could argue that each fact has degrees of certainty. However, it appears that some things have such a high degree of certainty, such as "real truths" referred to earlier, that we can be quite sure of those things being true. For example, we know with a high degree of certainty that two plus two equals four.

It does not matter whether we are is in China or on the moon. If we have two items and add two more items, we would have four items, regardless of what label we use to represent the number four. Also, if Jane is taller than Bill, and Bill is taller than Joe, a person knows with a high degree of certainty that Jane is taller than Joe. Moreover, if a woman jumps off a building, gravity causes her to fall to the earth.

Therefore, since these things have such high degrees of certainty, we might conclude that we can be quite sure, if not absolutely sure, of these facts. However, unless dealing with mathematics, logic, scientific concepts such as gravity, or facts such as we are now alive, we might find that many "truths" have a lesser degree of certainty and might be different for different people. These are the perceived real truths. Many beliefs are "true" because people perceive them as true, even when the beliefs have a low degree of certainty.

Truth-tests are tests which we might use to determine the truth of a fact or claim. There are several truth-tests such as Consensus Gentium — if all humans hold a belief, then it must be true — and Naïve Realism — only what can be directly observable by the individual is true. All the truth-tests appear to have deficiencies. However, the Correspondence, Coherence, and the Pragmatic-test appear to have the fewest deficiencies and seem the most useful to us. These three tests might be used to determine the truth of a fact or claim. We already apply these truth-tests to a certain degree whether we know it or not. Therefore, we might as well consciously use these tests to carefully and deliberately determine whether we should accept, reject, or suspend judgment about a fact or claim. If we find ourselves in the lower stratum, we might use these tests to discard disabling truths and to determine truths which work better for our lives.

The Correspondence-test requires that we check a fact/claim against a real object/event. If the fact/claim corresponds to the real world object/event, we consider the fact/claim to be true. For example, we could check the fact or claim that some force, whether called gravity or not, causes items to fall to the earth when dropped.

Figure 11.2 Sometimes we just don't know for sure.

Believe those who are seeking the truth. Doubt those who find it.
Andre Paul Guillaume Gide

Photo Caption

Our reality is perceived and distorted by our five senses and our brain.

Garland Sharp

Perception might not be reality, but it is all we have.
Garland Sharp

We could easily determine the truth of this fact/claim using the Correspondence-test. When we drop an item, and it falls to the earth, our subjective mental concept of gravity corresponds to the real object/event. Therefore, we consider this fact/claim true. We can also easily check the fact/claim that two plus two equals four. We could take two items and add two other items, and we would have four. Our subjective mental concept of two plus two equals four corresponds to the real world object/event of adding two items with two other items and then having four items.

When we move from concepts such as gravity and mathematics described as real truths, problems emerge with this test because the realty which we encounter is colored by perception. Our reality is only a representation of the real world object/event. Our definitions of self and our world determine what the reticular activating system (RAS) or the brain's filtering system allows us to detect. This definition of self and the world also helps to determine how we perceive what we detect. This colors our perception of the real world object/event.

As stated earlier, we suffer from selective detection and biased perception. We fail to detect all and then biasedly perceive what is detected in the world. Therefore, no mental concept is exactly like the real world object/event. However, if the fact/claim has a high degree of correspondence to the real world object/event such as gravity causing dropped objects to fall to the earth, we would consider the fact/claim as true. In contrast, if the fact/claim has a low degree of correspondence to the real world object/event such as witches causing illnesses, we would consider the fact/claim as false.

The Correspondence-test has other limitations. Because we find ourselves trapped in a single time and space, we cannot always check our mental concept against the real object/event. If the real world object/event is not directly accessible for observation, we have nothing real against which we can check our mental concept. We cannot check to see what happened in Rome in 12 AD, what happened in China today if we were not in China, or what happened to grandmother's soul when she died. However, if we wanted to test facts or claims such as gravity causing items to fall to the earth, we would find the Correspondence-test reliable.

The second test is the Coherence-test, which might be helpful in situations where we cannot directly check our mental concept with the real object/event. According to the Coherence-test, a fact or claim is accepted as true if it harmonizes (coheres) with other facts believed by the individual as true.

As we perceive or decode information from the environment, we determine whether it is true based on existing beliefs. If the fact or claim agrees with our established beliefs, we might accept the fact or claim as true. If the fact/claim fails to agree with our established beliefs, we might reject the fact/claim. We might use this test in determining the truth of what we read, which is said to have happened in Rome in 12 AD, or what happened in China today if we were not in China. If what we read coheres with our knowledge about Rome in 12 AD or our knowledge of China, we might consider what we read to be true. If what we read fails to cohere with the rest of our knowledge, we might consider what is read as false. If we read that the Romans or Chinese dropped fifty-pound items and the items failed to fall to the earth, we would probably reject this fact or claim. This would not cohere with our beliefs about gravity.

Pitfalls also exist with this test. If we compare and accept a new fact/claim based on existing beliefs which are false, this fact/claim could move us farther from real world objects/events. On the other hand, we might find that if the fact/claim fails to harmonize or cohere with our established beliefs, our reticular activating system could cause us to build a scotoma — or blind spot — to the fact/claim. Even if the fact/claim gets through, we might reject it, even if it exists in the real world. For example, a man might fail to believe that viruses cause his illness or that his oppressor causes his plight when these beliefs fail to cohere with his existing beliefs. In contrast, if the real or imagined fact/claim **does** harmonize or cohere with his existing beliefs, the RAS allows the information to get through to him to support the belief in the real or imagined fact/claim. He might accept the fact/claim even if it fails to exist in the real world — such as witches causing his illness or that Buddha causes his plight. With the Coherence-test, people could build a belief system far from reality.

The third test is the Pragmatic-test. With the Pragmatic-test, if the fact/claim (which could be a real or perceived real truth) works or brings about the desired results, then it is considered to be true. For example, if sick individuals pray to Allah for healing … and recover, the idea of Allah answering their prayers works for them. If other sick individuals pray to Buddha for healing … and recover, the idea of Buddha answering their prayers works for them. According to the Pragmatic-test, if the idea works, then it is true.

Problems exist with this test in terms of correspondence. Christian states, "For an idea or belief to work pragmatically we must believe it in terms of correspondence." For example, if we believe that Buddha answers our prayers, we must believe that a real object/event exists which corresponds to our mental concept of Buddha. Although we cannot prove that the object/event exists, we must believe that Buddha exists in terms of correspondence before we can believe that Buddha answers prayers on a pragmatic level.

You cannot depend on your eyes when your imagination is out of focus.

Mark Twain

…If there be any idea which, if believed in, would help us to lead a better life, then it would be really better for us to believe in that idea, unless, indeed, belief in it incidentally clashed with other greater vital benefits.

William James

Figure 11.3 The Buddha. If sick individuals pray to Buddha for healing … and recover, the idea of Buddha answering their prayers works for them. According to the Pragmatic-test, this is true for them.

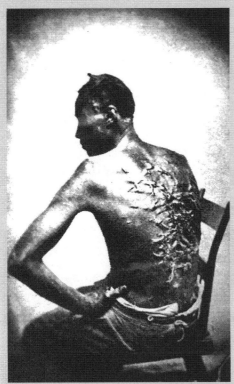

Figure 11.4 Scars of a whipped Mississippi slave. It is very hard to conceive that if the slave masters did not treat the slaves right that they taught the slaves right.

If they did this to his back, what do you think they did to his mind?

Rosanne Smith

As stated earlier, the three truth-tests have intrinsic problems. We cannot be absolutely certain of the results of any test. For example, with the Correspondence-test, we might mistake correlation for a cause. With the Coherence-test, we might accept a new fact/claim based on our existing erroneous beliefs. With the Pragmatic-test, we might find that something works, but fails to exist as a real world object/event. However, even with the intrinsic problems, we might use the tests to evaluate facts or claims. Brooke Moore and Richard Parker corroborate this notion and seem to have implied the use of the Correspondence-test and the Coherence-test. They state, "Generally speaking, it is reasonable to accept an unsupported claim (1) if it does not conflict with our own observation, our background information, or other credible claims and (2) if it comes from a credible source that offers us no reason to suspect bias." If analyzing the statements, first, we would find that it is reasonable to accept the claim if it does not conflict with our observations: the correspondence test. Second, we would accept if it does not conflict with our background information or other credible claims: the coherence-test.

Much has been said about the truth-tests, but little about credible, unbiased sources. For example, slaves or descendants of slaves should beware of facts and claims presented by the slave masters. The descendants of slaves must evaluate the biased source. They must beware of facts or claims presented by people who certified the slaves as non-human. Someone once said, "If they will not treat you right, what makes you think they will teach you right." If we are slaves or if we are in the lower stratum, we should beware of factual claims presented by the ones in the upper stratum — about such things as religion, history, and our self-worth. We should know that many of the factual claims are flat-out **lies**. Therefore, we should be careful of our gurus or mythmakers. Often, through myths or beliefs, mythmakers manipulate the environment to maintain the social order. They create and maintain illogical ideologies that support notions such as class, castes, and race. They use such things as religion, history, and laws to maintain the social order. They have instilled and continue to instill self-hate in its many forms in billions of people.

A fourth item should be added to Brooke Moore and Richard Parker's argument on accepting unsupported claims. It is reasonable to accept an unsupported claim if the claim works: the Pragmatic-test. However, individuals should be careful of this test. What works

If you tell the truth, you will have only one story to remember.
Barbie Scates

might not represent real world objects/events. A man might have believed that Buddha answered his prayers and caused him to be healed ... when in reality, Buddha did not answer his prayers. The fact might be that the man would have gotten well even if he had not prayed to Buddha.

> The sun will set without thy assistance.
> *The Talmud*

Since our truths help in determining our actions, we should choose empowering perceived real truths and discard disabling perceived real truths. Again, unless dealing with real truths such as mathematics or concepts such as gravity, many perceived real truths become effectively true because people believe them to be true, and the truths work for them. This can be seen with the beliefs by millions of individuals in the thousands of gods and religions throughout recorded history. Many times, the perceived real truths accepted by people work for them in negative ways — supporting their inferior status. In contrast, they could adopt different perceived real truths that could work for them in positive ways. They can and should discard the disempowering perceived real truths and adopt empowering truths to move them from self-hate to self-love and from false consciousness to class consciousness.

> I am not so concerned about people who refuse to think outside the box. I am concerned that people do not even think inside the box.
> *Garland Sharp*

We have to live today by what truth we can get today, and be ready tomorrow to call it falsehood.

William James

My doctors told me I would never walk again. My mother told me I would. I believed my mother.
Wilma Rudolph
The fastest woman on Earth in the 1960s

Chapter 12

Obstacles to Developing the Truth

Photo Caption

What a splendid
head, yet no brain.
Aesop

Figure 12.1 There were no crops this year. Are the gods punishing us for our sins?

Figure 12.2 If we strongly believe that a ladder has the power to cause bad luck, we might inadvertently do something to cause bad luck after walking under one.

In an attempt to develop TFB-characteristics that work effectively, if we are not careful, we might continue to engage in flawed thinking and deal unsuccessfully with several egocentric problems. These contribute to us having selective detection and biased perception (SDBP). If we fail to make corrections, these might stand in the way of using critical thinking and truth-tests to develop truths that work effectively for us. Although others exist, here are some of the most common flawed thinking patterns.

Illusory correlation is one such flawed thinking pattern. This is the belief that there is a correlation between events when no correlation exists. As stated earlier, when checking facts or claims using the Correspondence-test, if the subjective mental concept corresponds to the real world object/event, individuals might consider the fact or claim as true, or have a high degree of certainty. However, when checking the real world object/event against our subjective mental concept, we might mistake correlation for cause. For example, if we get cold and wet and then become sick from a cold, we might mistakenly believe that getting cold and wet caused the cold. Getting cold and wet might reduce our resistance to getting sick, but it is viruses which cause us to have a cold.

Illusory correlation forms the basis for many superstitions and irrational beliefs. For example, if a man walked under a ladder and then had bad luck, he might misapply the Correspondence-test and believe that the ladder caused the bad luck. If a man encountered a person believed to be a witch and the man became sick, he might believe that the perceived witch caused the illness. The ladder or the perceived witch has no power to cause people to experience bad luck or to get sick. However, if we define situations as real, they are real in their consequences. If we strongly believe that these have the power to cause sickness or bad luck, we might get sick after encountering a perceived witch or do something to cause bad luck after walking under a ladder.

A superstition is a premature explanation that overstays its time.
George Iles

Another flawed thinking pattern is belief perseverance, the tendency which we have to cling to our beliefs even when we find those beliefs false. For example, with belief perseverance, if a teacher believes that a student cannot do a certain task, and the student accomplishes the task, the teacher's RAS might filter out the accomplishment to maintain the belief she has about the student. If the teacher realizes the student has accomplished the task, the teacher might rationalize that the success was due to luck or an accident. The accomplishment fails to cohere with the established beliefs;

Superstition is the religion of feeble minds.

-Burke

Edmond Burke

therefore, it is rejected. The teacher holds on to her existing belief even if the belief is disproved. Therefore, through belief preservation, the first impression of a person by the observer might be very hard to change. This type of thinking could be detrimental to a perceived learning disabled child or a perceived inferior person.

Another flawed thinking pattern is confirmation bias, the tendency which we have to seek information that confirms our beliefs while overlooking information that conflicts with our beliefs. We sometimes seek information to confirm beliefs that are far from real world objects/events. Using confirmation bias, we might seek information to confirm already existing beliefs and reject information, using belief perseverance which contradicts these beliefs.

We accept new information as true using the Coherence-test, based on existing beliefs, which might cause us to go in vicious circles. For example, we might seek to confirm new erroneous beliefs with existing erroneous information. The new belief is accepted based on existing erroneous beliefs. This process stands in the way of critical thinking and aids us in building elaborate coherent belief systems that might be far from real world objects/events. The perceived witch or the ladder has no power to cause illnesses or bad luck, but we might seek examples which cohere with and confirm these beliefs. We also might seek out and associate with people who believe as we do. This also aids in confirming our existing beliefs.

The halo effect is another flawed thinking pattern which might occur when a good quality of an individual in one area influences our judgment of other qualities in the individual in different areas. We might mistakenly believe that a person competency in one area would make that person competent in another area. For example, Magic Johnson, one of the greatest basketball players ever, made a lousy coach. Managers sometimes mistakenly believe that an excellent worker on the production floor would make a good supervisor.

Simple causation might be added to the list of flawed thinking patterns. This occurs when we believe that a single factor caused an effect, instead of a combination of contributing factors. For example, we might believe that a certain person became wealthy because of hard work. But, several factors caused the person to become wealthy. We might believe that a person is impoverished because of racism. However, there are other factors in addition to racism which contribute to the person's status.

We face certain egocentric conditions simply because of being human. These conditions, together with flawed thinking patterns, if not handled correctly, deter us from critical thinking and using truth-tests to develop truths that correspond closely to real world objects/events. One such condition is the egocentric trap. We know that we find ourselves trapped in a single time and a single space. We can only observe the world from this condition. We cannot observe all that goes on in the world. Therefore, the egocentric trap causes us to develop and maintain our TFB-characteristics based on limited information.

As stated earlier, not only are we capable of observing only part of the world from a single time and space but because of the egocentric trap, we also have egocentric or selective detection. Christian states, "The mind selects a few elements of any object/event to assimilate into the model that will be used for thinking." This aids us in understanding egocentric or selective detection. We select only bits of what we are capable of observing, to use for thinking, and because of the egocentric predicament, we interpret it based on existing biases. Therefore, we develop, maintain, and change our TFB-characteristics based mostly on limited, biased information.

What Perry describes as the egocentric predicament mentioned above, might be added to the list. We find ourselves trapped in a body and cannot experience the world apart from biased perception. Even if we tried to experience the world apart from biased perception, we still face the egocentric trap and egocentric or selective detection. We find ourselves trapped in a single time and space, and we only experience pieces of what goes on in the world. Also, our mind selects only pieces of what we are capable of observing, to be used for thinking.

Christian describes another egocentric condition as the egocentric illusion, which might also be added to the list. This illusion entails the belief that the entire universe revolves around us, at our point in space and time. We believe that we are the center of the universe. Christian believes that if we fail to correct for the egocentric illusion and feel that we are the center of the universe ... and feel that others should treat us as such, we suffer from aristocentrism, an unjustified claim to superiority. We can see where notions such as royalty, racism, and caste systems could follow from such thinking.

The fifth egocentric condition, which we call the egocentric fallacy, causes us to believe that what we experience through our perceptual and information-processing faculties, is exactly like the real world object/event, or is 100 % true. This might be the most insidious of the egocentric conditions. We fail to recognize that what we experience is just a representation of the world. Our representation in many cases is, quite different from that of others. We fail to recognize that most "truths" have degrees of probability of being true. The egocentric fallacy can lead to a host of problems when we strongly believe that others' experiences and beliefs fail to represent real world objects/events when they are different from our experiences and beliefs.

Figure 12.3 Manhole cover, pinpointing the Center of the Universe in Wallace, Idaho by Jan Kronsell/Wikimedia Commons/ CC BY-SA 3.0

Patriotism is your conviction that this country is superior to all other countries because you were born in it.
George Bernard Shaw

Photo Caption

Reality is merely an illusion, albeit a very persistent one.
Albert Einstein

Figure 12.4 Alexej von Jawlensky *Die Sinnende* — in English: *The thinking woman.* If we do not think, others will do our thinking for us. "THINK"

If we fail to deal effectively with the egocentric conditions, we might be deterred from critical thinking and effectively using truth-tests. This aids in building and maintaining beliefs that fail to correspond with the real world object/event. We must realize that what we observe and believe about the world is based on our interpretation of the world. It is only a representation of the real world object or event, based on our limited and biased sensory experiences. As discussed earlier, our sensory experiences come from transducers such as eyes, nose, and ears ... transmitting the physical world to us. We then interpret this data.

Because "reality" is based on our interpretation of the sensory experiences from our transducers, people in different cultures may interpret reality differently. We might add that because of our interpretation of our sensory experiences from our transducers, people in the same culture may also interpret reality differently.

If we deal effectively with the errors in thinking and the egocentric conditions, we might use critical thinking and truth-tests to aid us in evaluating and developing truths that have higher probabilities of corresponding to real world objects/events. We could develop truths that work more effectively for ourselves which aid in eliminating our self-limiting beliefs.

You act and feel not according to what things are really like, but according to the image your mind holds of what they are like. You have a certain mental image of yourself, your world, and the people around you, and you behave as though these images were truth, the reality, rather than the things they represent.
Maxwell Maltz

Chapter 13

Developing Truths that Work

The man who acquires the ability to take full possession of his mind may take possession of anything else to which he is justly entitled.

Andrew Carnegie

I'm not sure I want popular opinion on my side—I've noticed those with the most opinions often have the fewest facts.
Bethania McKenstry

"You ain't goin' no where ... son. You ought to go back to driving a truck."
Jim Denny of the Grand Ole Opry to Elvis Presley

We should take the time to define or redefine ourselves, adopting truths that work best for us, while rejecting disabling truths. Remember that real truth such as 2 + 2 = 4 should be accepted. However, if we fail to define perceived real truths, others will define these truths for us. People such as religious leaders, teachers, and politicians define these truths and expect individuals to believe and accept the defined truths. We should be careful of the truth — or popular opinion — of the society. We should be wary of Consensus Gentium: If all humans hold the belief, then it must be true.

If we find that a perceived real truth of the society is empowering, we might adopt that truth. If we find that perceived real truth is disabling, we might reject that truth. We should be willing to change our truths over time. Our truths, today, might be false tomorrow. Most people no longer believe that the earth is flat, or that Jupiter rules the heavens. These beliefs had powerful effects on countless people's thinking and actions in the past. Sailors sailed only so far out to sea in fear of falling off the edge of the earth. People made sacrifices to Jupiter. Individuals who worshipped Jupiter probably believed in Jupiter as strongly as Christians presently believe in Christ or Muslims presently believe in Allah.

We should adopt truths which empower us and others, even if the truths contradict the prevailing beliefs of our society. If the conventional wisdom or belief of the society is not a real truth — such as an object falls to the earth when dropped or two plus two equals four — the belief might need close examination. We might examine the conventional wisdom of our society carefully especially if we find ourselves on the bottom rung. Although no outcast may ever read this book, the whole notion of writing about class, caste, and racist systems is to show the fallacies of ideologies and systems in societies, hoping that people might recognize the fallacies of their ideologies and systems.

The dominant beliefs socialized into individuals are beliefs preferred by the ruling stratum. Just because most of the people in the society believe a certain thing ... does **not** necessarily mean that it has a high probability of representing real world objects/events appropriately. For example, if a billion Muslims believe that Allah is God, and there is no God but Allah, does that make it right? A billion Christians might disagree. Therefore, we should stop swallowing disabling socialized beliefs such as unworthiness. We should reject

The most radical revolutionary will become a conservative the day after the revolution.
Hannah Arendt

the reality of being inferior and deserving the status of poor or outcast. We can then redefine ourselves, knowing that everyone is fundamentally the same. By accident, not by the will of God, we were born into a certain status in life or with a certain skin color.

> When men destroy their old gods, they will find new ones to take their place.
> *Pearl Buck*

> The reining in of expectations was the centerpiece of the outside world's overall message, and it came through loud and clear. Limits had been defined, had been written into law and forcefully advised to understand and accept that the burden would always be on me to see to it that my dreams were tailored to fit such width and breadth as the limited expectations assigned me could comfortably entertain. While "expectations" meant "the sky's the limit" for those favored, that interpretation should never be expected to apply in cases like mine. I listened intently until each point had been driven home. Then I said, "Fu… you," in the nicest way I could.
>
> *Sidney Poitier*

My child, there is a sea … nay! … a veritable ocean of humanity out there … and you probably won't be able to relate to any of them.

At the guru's feet by Grea, Sangrea.net /CC-BY-ND-3.0

Figure 13.1 We should be careful of our gurus, and the conventional wisdom of the society.

> As another has well said, to handicap a student by teaching him that his black face is a curse and that his struggle to change his condition is hopeless is the worst sort of lynching.
>
> Carter G. Woodson

If we desire to be or do more, we might require changes to our truth about ourselves and the world. We may find these changes difficult, but worth the effort. For example, feelings of inferiority might be difficult to shed for many black individuals in America who grew up in the South during the 50s and 60s. Socialization and conditioning caused them to internalize the "truth" that blacks were inferior to whites. Growing up seeing the water fountains and bathrooms labeled "Colored" and "White," being required to go to the back doors of restaurants, and required to go to the back of the bus, contributed to making blacks feel inferior to whites.

The segregated black schools which used the old textbooks that were discarded by the white schools, and seeing blacks on television shown in negative roles, further contributed to causing them to feel inferior to whites. This "truth" has affected many black individuals, causing them to be predictable and live for many years far below their potential. This feeling of inferiority to whites plagued your author for years. Attending the University of Tennessee aided in reversing this feeling of inferiority. A sociology course that used the text by Ian Robertson entitled *Sociology* exposed the notion of race as a false or disempowering "truth." It changed your author's belief that whites were better or superior to blacks. Eventually, he accepted that one mythical race being better than another mythical race — based on skin color — did not make **good nonsense**, let alone good sense. His beliefs about race ceased to be a limitation.

Figure 13.2 Colored Waiting Room Sign. Blacks having to wait in the Colored waiting room lowered the self-esteem of blacks in the South.

Photo Caption

Even if we have limitations, and everyone does, we might be able to convince ourselves otherwise. For example, if a man tells the big lie long enough, people tend to believe the lie. Therefore, if he tells himself a new truth and visualizes the new truth, even if it has a low probability of being true long enough, he might tend to believe and convince others of the new truth. If he tells himself the "truth" repeatedly, he might come to believe and act on that "truth." For example, he could tell himself and visualize himself as wealthy even if he does not have much money. He could tell himself and visualize himself as fifty pounds lighter before he loses the weight. Then he could begin to act and think like a wealthy or slimmer person. The man tells himself the new "truth" and acts and thinks as a wealthy or slimmer person before he obtains wealth or loses the weight.

I spent twenty years in the South one night.
Dick Gregory

A lie told often enough becomes the truth.

Lenin

Although we might sometimes need to adopt truths that contradict the prevailing beliefs of our society, this does not advocate such things as going naked in the streets or committing crimes which harm others. Yes, there might be a good reason for the road less traveled. Without some basic and agreed-upon truths, neither the society nor the individual could survive. Hopefully, we will build our truths on the notion of lifting ourselves and others above the lower stratum, to new and better ways of being human.

Figure 13.3 There might be a good reason for the road less traveled.

PART FOUR

A BETTER WAY OF BEING HUMAN

Chapter 14

Removing Your Foot From Your Neck

In the light of this truth, what, then, is the meaning of "fighting against circumstances?" It means that a man is continually revolting against an effect without, while all the time he is nourishing and preserving its cause in his heart.

James Allen

Figure 14.1 It is hard to get ahead when people have their feet on your neck.

Figure 14.2 Condemned to Agony. People might become frustrated because of their inability to change themselves and their world due to the feet on their necks. They might feel they are condemned to agony.

During a discussion between the author and a frustrated friend at work who had just been passed over for a promotion, she remarked, "It is hard to get ahead when people have their feet on your neck." Even if she has high self-esteem, a positive self-image, feelings of worthiness, and has adopted class consciousness, she might still find difficulty in producing positive change. When individuals in the lower stratum decide to change or re-socialize themselves, they must deal with several feet on their necks.

They have to deal with their own feet, the big feet of the ruling stratum, the feet of others in their environments such as parents and peers, and the big feet of gods. To people such as outcasts in India, the fourth generation of poor unwed moms in America, and even ourselves, change might seem insurmountable. Overcoming our self-limiting beliefs and re-socializing ourselves may not be as overwhelming as overcoming the misaligned feelings of being nurtured as the opposite sex, like the boy described by Dr. Belinda Trotter. However, overcoming our self-limiting beliefs and re-socializing ourselves may not be as easy as just seeing the true nature of our plight in an oppressed group, and questioning our social arrangement in the system.

As stated earlier, three of the reasons systems or ideologies such as castes, class, and racism remain powerful are because the ruling stratum controls the resources necessary to preserve the system, people generally believe throughout the society that the inequality is natural and right, and many individuals spend their time — sometimes without success — satisfying their basic survival needs. Therefore, we might become frustrated because of our inability to change ourselves and our world due to the feet on our neck.

How can the outcast in India be re-socialized and shed the belief of being an outcast and become a productive member of the society? How can the fourth generation of poor unwed mothers stop the nonsense and cause the next generation to have wealth instead of poverty? How can poor individuals with low self-esteem in America, England, or India discard the notion of inferiority and be more successful?

To change and re-socialize ourselves, we must first remove our own feet from our neck. As stated earlier, a person administers most social controls internally without much direct external control. Therefore, we should realize that no god requires us to live in the lower stratum. We should adopt class consciousness and realize that we are responsible for our lives. It is not the government or the gods, but mainly ourselves, who are responsible for our success or failure. We must identify our present and desired condition, and then identify strategies and set appropriate goals to move us toward the desired conditions.

We are each responsible for our own life—no other person is or ever can be.

Oprah Winfrey

In order to win, you must expect to win.

Richard Bach

No matter how hard you work for success, if your thought is saturated with the fear of failure, it will kill your efforts, neutralize your endeavors, and make success impossible.

Baudjuin

A man only begins to be a man when he ceases to whine and revile, and commences to search for the hidden justice which regulates his life. And as he adapts his mind to that regulating factor, he ceases to accuse others as the cause of his condition, and builds himself up in strong and noble thoughts.

James Allen

Brian Tracy, in his book entitled *Maximum Achievement*, states that success equals goals, and all else is commentary. However, if we have our own feet on our neck, this might inhibit us from setting and reaching our goals. When we fail to eliminate our self-limiting or hypnotized beliefs and negative emotions, our feet remain on our necks.

Even if we set and work on empowering goals, our self-limiting beliefs, and negative emotions could cause us to work against ourselves, similar to hypnotized subjects when told they cannot lift a pencil. Worse yet, our feet on our necks might cause us to avoid working on our goals … or even cause us to fail to set goals.

In most cases, we remain in inferior statuses mainly because of our own feet on our neck. Our greatest obstacle is often ourselves. We need to dehypnotize ourselves and shed our self-limiting beliefs and negative emotions, thereby removing our feet from our neck. If we do not change our self-limiting beliefs, we might be like the boy nurtured as the opposite sex, described previously by Belinda Trotter. Even if everyone treats the boy as a boy and he sees himself in the mirror with the features of a boy, he still feels like a girl. For example, a man might say that he desires wealth and success while clinging to the inner belief that it is hard for a rich man to get into heaven. This type of thinking, if consistently done, neutralizes his actions and makes attaining wealth virtually impossible.

With some introspection, we might begin to shed our self-limiting beliefs when we realize that many of these beliefs have a low probability of being true. Sometimes with great pain, we might have to shed cherished self-limiting beliefs which have worked for us for a long time. This might require us to radically change our thinking about such things as racism, caste systems, royalty, and religion.

If we want to rid ourselves of our self-limiting socialized beliefs, we might take an approach similar to that of Rene Descartes, who in his quest to find the "truth" proceeded to doubt everything. He states in his writing of *Meditations,* "Several years have now elapsed since I first became aware that I had accepted, even from my youth, many false opinions for true, and that consequently what I afterward based on such principles was highly doubtful; and from that time I was convinced of the necessity of undertaking once in my life to rid myself of all the opinions I had adopted, and of commencing anew the work of building from the foundation, if I desired to establish a firm and abiding superstructure in the sciences."

We might disagree about whether this approach worked well for Descartes. But, today we have much more scientific information to work with than Descartes. We have a better chance of developing

Figure 14.3 Rene Descartes

If you would be a real seeker after truth, it is necessary that at least once in your life you doubt, as far as possible, all things.

Rene Descartes

Courage is being scared to death — but saddling up anyway.

John Wayne

truths closer to real world objects/events, instead of believing that "gods" cause everything. We might not examine every belief that we have had since childhood, although this seems to be a good idea. However, at a minimum, in our quest for truth or things having a high probability of being true, we should critically examine our worldview and identify the many false opinions or disabling truths which we have accepted as true. We might take the time to list on paper these false opinions or disabling truths to be critically examined. After critical examination, if we find ourselves dissatisfied with our lives, we should immediately discard the many false opinions that cause us to have our own feet on our neck.

> The unexamined life is not worth living.
> *Socrates*

Along with unworthiness, we must discard other negative emotions such as fear, jealously, envy and guilt, if we are to remove our feet from our neck. We should immediately discard these emotions. These emotions, intertwined with our other self-limiting beliefs, will keep us from moving ahead. For example, we might fear failure because we fail to believe that we can accomplish a desired task or goal. We might also fear success for reasons such as believing that we might not be able to maintain the success, or we might not want to accept the responsibilities that come with success. In either case, whether we fear failure or success, we fail to make progress mainly because of our own feet on our neck.

In some cases, simply doing what we fear causes the fear to dissipate. Of course, we might have justifiable fears, but most jealousy, envy, and guilt serve no good purpose. If we critically examine our feelings of envy and jealousy, we would probably find that these serve no good purpose and should be immediately tossed out. Guilt — at times — serves the person, if it causes remorse for doing something believed to be wrong. However, after that, it should be tossed out.

As discussed earlier, worthiness appears to be one of the keys to success and happiness. Guilt can hamper a person from feeling worthy. If we do or have done things which make us feel guilty, or if we retain any of the negative emotions, they hinder us. We should right the wrongs in our lives and practice forgiving ourselves and others. We must first forgive ourselves. Then we should forgive others for all the wrongs committed against us by others. We need to forgive ourselves and the world, and then stop behaviors which cause us to feel guilty if we believe the behaviors are wrong. But, if the guilt stems from our fallacious conditioning and the many false

Man is buffeted by circumstances so long as he believes himself to be the creature of outside conditions. But when he realizes that he may command the hidden soil and seeds of his being out of which circumstances grow, he then becomes the rightful master of himself.

James Allen

opinions accepted as true, we should change how we perceive the behaviors. For example, our conditioning — or the people in the environment — could cause us to feel guilty doing things that might be beneficial to us ... such as striving to be wealthy, or marrying a person of a different class, caste, or mythical race.

Individuals with "big feet" use guilt to keep people in the lower stratum. People in the lower stratum should examine the beliefs that make them feel guilty and decide whether the beliefs are wrong or not. Not wrong because the ones with the big feet or people in their society **say** it is wrong but wrong because they believe it is wrong after critical examination and introspection.

We should strive to replace our negative emotions with positive emotions such as joy, peace, love — and, of course, worthiness. If we love ourselves, we could rid ourselves of unworthiness. Love might well be the greatest of the positive emotions. Also, if all people would love their neighbor as themselves, many of the woes of the world would disappear. If we treated others as we would like to be treated, there would be no caste, class, or racist systems. Therefore, we should have the courage to rid ourselves of the many false opinions and negative emotions.

Once we remove our feet from our neck by ridding ourselves of the many false opinions and negative emotions, we can adopt more empowering beliefs and positive emotions. We can then deal more effectively with the external big feet. We should find our ability to make changes easier without our own feet on our neck.

Chapter 15

Removing External Big Feet

It should be apparent by now that of all the feet on our necks, the most important feet to remove are our own feet. We cannot over-emphasize the fact that people administer most social controls internally without much direct external influence. Our beliefs about ourselves outweigh the beliefs of others towards us and any external control in the environment. With the proper TFB-characteristics, we can usually overcome the outside influences. Yet, it would be a mistake for us to underestimate the power of others with big feet. Even if a woman removes her foot from her neck, adopts new truths, and identifies strategies to bring about change, she might still find change difficult.

First, people should not underestimate the power of the ruling stratum with the big feet which controls the resources necessary to maintain the system. The ruling stratum has the power to create powerful systems for social control. For example, in many countries such as Saudi Arabia, the ruling class or the people with the big feet created — and some still help maintain — a monarchy/royalty system. This system aided and still aids in controlling the masses.

He who is in power controls the "truth."
Garland Sharp

In countries such as India, the upper caste — or the people with the big feet — created, and some still help maintain, a caste system that aided and still aids in controlling millions of people in rural India. In America, the notion of royalty and outcasts might seem far-fetched to many people, but they have accepted and still accept the ideology of racism. Powerful people with the big feet created and some still support the ideology of racism which in the past enslaved, and today still stratifies, millions of people.

Although some blacks such as President Obama, Oprah Winfrey, and Bob Johnson have reached the upper stratum in America, racism in America keeps millions of black people in the lower stratum thus maintaining the stratification of the society. Therefore, people should not underestimate the power of the individuals with the big feet. They create powerful systems and ideologies which aid in maintaining stratification.

As discussed earlier, it is hard for us to excel when someone has their feet on our neck. To further see the vast power of the ruling stratum with the big feet and their lasting effects, we simply need to look at slavery and imperialism. For example, even when individuals no longer have the ruling stratum's feet on their neck in the form of slavery and imperialism, the impact of the feet can last for generations. The devastating effects of slavery in America have lasted for generations and still affect millions of people. Such also is the case with imperialism; it has had and is still having devastating effects on the lives of millions of people. We need only compare the European colonized countries with the one which they failed to colonize. Japan, the only major country in the Third World that the Europeans failed to colonize was the first to become an economic power. Chomsky corroborates this notion. He states in the book entitled *The Prosperous Few and the Restless Many*, "Japan fended off colonization almost entirely; that's why Japan is the one area of the Third World that developed. That's striking. The one part of the Third World that wasn't colonized is the one part that's part of the industrialized world. That's not by accident. To strengthen the point, you need only look at the parts of Europe that were colonized. Those parts — like Ireland — are much like the Third World. The patterns are striking. So when people in the Third World blame the history of imperialism for their plight, they have a very strong case to make."

The Europeans did not have their feet on the necks of the Japanese as they did the people in the other countries in the so-called Third World. We know that China is emerging. Yet, Japan became an economic power long before China. Ireland and the Third World countries still feel the effects of imperialism. To further strengthen this point, we need only look at Bangladesh, the first country colonized. Bangladesh is one of the poorest, if not the poorest, country in the world. So when people in the so-called Third World and Ireland blame the history of imperialism for their plight, they do have a strong case to make.

The ruling stratum also controls or influences the agents used to socialize us. Therefore, we should not underestimate the power of others in our environment with big feet such as family members, friends, religious leaders, and teachers. These people, who make up the institutions in the society, aid in socializing individuals to conform to the systems preferred by the ruling stratum. The socialization agents helped to socialize and continue to socialize people throughout their lives. As discussed earlier, most of us internalize the socialized TFB-characteristics and uncritically conform to them. Then, we avoid change without much direct influence. If we attempt to change, people such as family members, friends, religious leaders, and teachers seek to prevent us from changing. Other people with the big feet sometimes are well meaning. But, they want us to be predictable and stay where we belong. This is like the blind leading the blind. It takes courage for us to change when these people have their feet on our neck.

If the powerful systems and ideologies such as castes, class, and racism, along with the socializing agents, fail to cause us to conform, the ones with the big feet have other methods to cause conformity. The individuals in power with the big feet might give non-conformists negative labels and use the media, schools, and any means necessary to spread propaganda about the dissenters. For example, if people speak out against a war waged by America or

Figure 15.1 The Parable of the Blind Leading the Blind by Abel Grimmer. In Mathew 15:14 it states that "And if the blind lead the blind, both shall fall into the ditch."

try to gain equality, they might be labeled as Communist, anti-American, or as public enemy number one. If these methods fail to cause us to conform, the ones with the big feet control the laws and the jails. They might use Jim Crow type laws to keep people segregated or use prisons to control dissenters.

Figure 15.2 Whites used Jim Crow-type laws to keep people segregated.

The prisons help to maintain stratification. For example, over two million people currently find themselves incarcerated in America's prisons and jails. In 2014 black males made up about 37% of America's male prison population according to the U.S. Department of Justice. We might find the percentage strange when blacks only represent about 13% of the total American population. Even when released from prison, these people, both black and white, find difficulty in obtaining a well-paying job. In many cases, they become disenfranchised which aids in keeping them in the lower stratum.

With all the feet on people's necks, they might find change difficult, if not impossible. As Chomsky stated, "So when people in the Third World blame the history of imperialism for their plight, they have a very strong case to make." When blacks in America blame the history of slavery and racism for their plight, they have a strong case to make. When the impoverished people of England blame their plight on the history of class, they have a strong case to make. When the outcasts of India blame their plight on the history of the Caste system, they have a strong case to make. With the devastating effects of systems, ideologies, and practices such as castes, racism, and imperialism coupled with the other feet on people's necks, we can see why billions of people conform to the TFB-characteristics of the society ... and why the stratification remains. Can we totally blame the outcast for being an outcast? Can we totally blame the poor person for being impoverished? Can we totally blame the black person for feeling inferior?

Although we who blame history and existing circumstances for our plight might have a very strong case to make, this fails to empower us. We might not be able to change our history or our current conditions, but we can change our attitudes toward these.

Everyone in Germany is a National Socialist — the few outside the party are either lunatics or idiots.
Adolf Hitler

It's not that they cared so much about my criminal record, just that they reckoned if I was dumb enough to get caught then I wasn't smart enough for the job.

Figure 15.3 Even when released from prison, people find difficulty in obtaining a well-paying job, which aids in keeping them in the lower stratum.

Figure 15.4 If Blacks blame history for their plight, they have a very strong case to make.

Figure 15.5 George Bernard Shaw. Shaw believed that people should not blame circumstances for what they are.

People are always blaming their circumstances for what they are. I don't believe in circumstances. The people who get on in this world are the people who get up and look for the circumstances they want, and, if they can't find them, make them.

George Bernard Shaw

Therefore, it seems that some change is possible for us under any condition. We might find change difficult, but the rewards outweigh the effort.

Sometimes we can change immediately, and at other times we change gradually. Some of us can just decide to change. Sometimes we change because of new information, or we change because of the realization that our beliefs fail to work for us anymore. In either case, our old ways of thinking might seem far-fetched. The outcast in India or the impoverished person in America could decide that all of the stuff about castes and God's will for them to be poor fail to make sense and discard the beliefs.

Many of us also immediately change when we adopt new definitions of ourselves and our world. For example, sometimes we immediately change when we accept Christ and define ourselves as Christians or as saved individuals. We immediately start acting like Christians. We accept a different role and accept the rules for the role. When we marry, we take on the role of marriage. As soon as we say, "I do," most of us act in different ways compared with single individuals. We now define ourselves as married, and take on the role of marriage.

We might witness drastic changes in ourselves when some guru or person in authority declares us saved or pronounces us married. If the preacher declares us saved or pronounces us married, then we immediately take on the role of being saved or married. We can have this same power over ourselves. We should be the **guru** or person in authority in our lives. We should pronounce or declare desired conditions or roles in our lives and redefine ourselves, then adopt the new conditions or roles. As the married or saved person, we should immediately start acting out the new roles.

Figure 15.6 Mildred and Garland Sharp at their Marriage. When the preacher pronounced them married, they immediately took on the role of being married.

We can redefine the "self" and adopt new roles, bringing about some changes immediately. Other changes come gradually and require us to control our socialization or re-socialization, to deal with the feet on our necks. We might employ the same agents used for socialization to re-socialize ourselves. We may begin to re-socialize ourselves when we recognize the many false opinions accepted as true and discard these opinions. If we are in the lower stratum, we must recognize that much of our socialization caused us to accept many opinions of the society that enabled us and the society to survive. However, we might want to strive to survive more comfortably in the upper stratum.

The socialization process does not stop when we become adults. The socialization process continues throughout our lifetime. Just as children do, adults are still evolving. As with children, adults perceive the environment and create definitions. These definitions then influence the adults' perception when creating other definitions.

To direct our socialization or re-socialization, it might require that we control or change our environment. Because the feedback from the environment aids in our socialization, it might be difficult for us to make positive changes while immersed in a disempowering environment. Our environment affects our thinking and behaviors. Therefore, we should redefine ourselves and strive to create an environment conducive to success. We should then allow our RAS to filter or block the disempowering parts of the environment which we might not be able to change. To do this, we should keep our minds focused on what we want, and off of the things which we do not want. We might set goals for "change" and stay focused on these goals.

Drawn by Charles Slay

Figure 15.7 The Scarecrow. The scarecrow was empowered to use his brain by the Wizard of Oz.

The scarecrow had brains before he met the Wizard of Oz.
Garland Sharp

The whole point of being alive is to evolve into the complete person you were intended to be.
Oprah Winfrey

Love thy neighbor as yourself, but choose your neighborhood.
Louise Beal

We do not know, in most cases, how far social failure and success are due to heredity, and how far to environment. But environment is the easier of the two to improve.
J. B. S. Haldane

You are a product of your environment. So choose the environment that will best develop you toward your objective. Analyze your life in terms of its environment. Are the things around you helping you toward success or are they holding you back?
W. Clement Stone

The greatest discovery of my generation is that a human being can alter his life by altering his attitudes of mind.

William James

You are always free to change your mind and choose a different future, or a different past.

Richard Bach

As stated earlier, the four main agents for socialization are the family, school, peers, and the media. We might use these agents along with the other socialization agents to re-socialize ourselves. We know that the socialization and learning processes usually start with the caregiver or family, and from the caregiver or family, we learn primarily through conditioning, language, and observation. Therefore, we may want to examine what we have previously and are currently learning, especially from our caregivers or parents. We should determine whether the information empowers us, or not. If we find our parents or care-givers' teaching dis-empowering, we should immediately toss it out. In many cases, it has been detrimental to us.

Many dysfunctional families have created dysfunctional individuals with negative emotions. We should not let the negative emotions of the past keep us captive. Although we cannot change the parent who gave us birth, we can change our opinion or attitude toward those parents. For example, growing up with a father who was sometimes abusive to others, and who spent little time with the author during his childhood, caused him to resent his father long after his father had died.

One day it dawned on the author that his father might have done the best he could with what he knew. The perception held by the author of his father changed. The negative feeling toward his father dissipated. Feelings of admiration replaced the feelings of resentment toward his father. These feelings have been more empowering. This shows that one can change one's mind and, effectively, choose a different past.

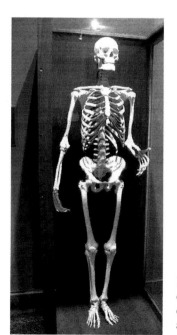

If you cannot get rid of the family skeleton, you may as well make it dance.

George Bernard Shaw

Figure 15.8 Everyone has skeletons in their closets, but as Richard Bach stated in the book entitled *Illusions*, "you can change your mind and choose a different past."

Photo Caption

As a general rule, the most successful man in life is the man who has the best information.

Benjamin Disraeli

Don't stay long when the husband is not at home.

Japanese Proverb

Because schools aid in our socialization, we can gain additional information for change through schools for re-socialization. For example, attending the Sociology and Philosophy classes at the University of Tennessee proved to be a defining moment for your author. These classes helped transform many of the erroneous beliefs he held. If not for these classes, this book might not have been written or published. These classes helped him to view the world differently. They helped him shed self-limiting beliefs and aided him in the removal of some "external feet."

We can change based on additional information gained through schools and new experiences. Therefore, we should be lifelong learners. We should understand the society and history of the TFB-characteristics accepted in the society. If we do not understand systems and ideologies such as caste, class, and racism, many other things will fail to make sense.

Neely Fuller corroborates this notion when he talks about racism. He states that "if you do not understand White Supremacy (Racism) — what it is, and how it works — everything else that you understand, will only confuse you." Therefore, if blacks do not understand racism and its evolution, if outcasts do not understand the caste system and its evolution, and if the impoverished person in England does not understand class and its evolution, many other things might not make sense. If they begin to understand the system or ideology and move away from false consciousness, they will begin to understand why caste members, the so-called lower class, and impoverished blacks do what they do to remain in the lower stratum. They might begin to understand why many people accept the reality presented to them. Therefore, knowledge is a key component in re-socialization.

In re-socializing ourselves, we might change our peer group. For example, if a man wants to stop committing adultery, he might rid himself of his girlfriend. If he has a problem with alcohol, he might avoid places where people drink alcohol. He should choose friends and peers that empower him. He should join clubs and organizations which empower him and uplift others. Also, to counteract the people with their feet on his neck, he might find a support group in the environment. This could be in the form of a mastermind group or a think tank. Napoleon Hill, in the Book *Think and Grow Rich,* discusses forming a mastermind group, which seems to be a good idea. Hill describes this mastermind group as a small group of well-meaning individuals who meet once a week to discuss ideas. The author was a member of a think tank that met regularly to discuss ideas. Even if we do not form a mastermind group or a think tank, we might need someone with whom we can discuss ideas.

I do not expect the white media to create positive black male images.

Huey Newton

Not Strong Enough.

Figure 15.9 You might not be young or strong enough to attain some goals. A dwarf, no matter how talented in basketball, should not spend most of his time practicing and aspiring to be a center in the National Basketball Association (NBA).

In directing our socialization, we should be careful of the media. As the media aids in socializing the child, the media continue to aid in controlling and socializing the adult. Why would anyone spend millions of dollars for a short commercial during the Super Bowl? The media have a tremendous power to influence the TFB-characteristics of individuals. Therefore, when seeking to re-socialize ourselves, we might want to avoid spending a lot of time watching television and swallowing the conventional wisdom of the day. The conventional wisdom of the day passed on by the media usually, aids in maintaining the status quo. This could be disabling for people in the lower stratum. However, some social media is beneficial.

Social media such as Facebook and YouTube can be extremely beneficial in gaining information to re-socialize oneself. For example, on YouTube, we can find people who are not puppets to conventional wisdom ... such as Francis Cress Welsing, Neil Degrasse Tyson, and Noam Chomsky. The Egyptian activist Wael Ghonim credited Facebook with the success of the Egyptian revolution that caused Hosni Mubarak to relinquish his power. Hitler is purported to have said, "What luck for rulers that men do not think." However, media such as Facebook and YouTube allow us to become better thinkers and to have access to others who are critical thinkers. Therefore, these types of media can be extremely beneficial.

People can direct their socialization, although sometimes it is with great difficulty. If raised in the ghettos or as the opposite sex, directing their re-socialization might seem extremely difficult or impossible. Yet, if even one other person has successfully changed the situation, the possibility for others to change the situation exists. If we want to achieve a goal or become a certain way, we should ask if anyone else under the same circumstances achieved that goal or became that way.

Again, if one other person has achieved it, the possibility exists for others. If many people have achieved a goal, not only does the possibility exist, but the probability of achieving the goal is greater. Even if no one has ever achieved it, the probability of us achieving the goal may be low, but the possibility might still exist. However, this does not suggest that everyone can do everything or reach any goal. We must have the talent and ability to do certain things. We might find some goals virtually impossible. For example, a man might find being the heavyweight boxing champion of the world at age 65 as virtually impossible. However, it might be possible for a younger man with the right hereditary blueprint, disposition, and desire to be the champion. A dwarf, no matter how talented in basketball, should not spend most of his time practicing and aspiring to be a center in the National Basketball Association (NBA). This would be highly improbable or virtually impossible.

Figure 15.10 President Barack Obama.
Things that might have been highly improbable in America twenty years ago are possible today. President Obama's election to the U.S. Presidency for two terms is a good example of this.

As mentioned earlier, while people who blame history and existing circumstances for their plight might have a very strong case to make, this generally fails to empower them. One can rise above caste. For example, Kocheril Raman Narayanan, an outcast, became the 10th president of India. One can rise above class. Jack Case, a machinist/toolmaker, became the Plant Manager of a Nuclear Facility employing over eight thousand people when there were thousands of people there who were more formally educated.

We can rise above racism. Things that had been highly improbable regarding race in America twenty years ago are possible today. We can turn to politics and sports for examples. Barack Obama became the first African American President of the United States in 2009 and was re-elected in 2012. A few weeks after Barack Obama became the first African American President in 2009, Michael Steele, an African American, became the National Chairman of the Republican Party. A few days later after Steele became the Chairman, Mike Tomlin, an African American, became the youngest coach ever to coach in and win the Super Bowl.

Blaming history for our plight might make a very good case, but this fails to empower us. Like Kocheril Raman Narayanan, Jack Case, and Barack Obama, we should shed the excuse of blaming history or any other outside circumstances for our plight, and start each day building a better life. An old African proverb might sum this up. The proverb states, "Every morning in Africa a gazelle wakes up and knows that it will have to outrun the fastest lion, or it will be killed. And every morning in Africa a lion wakes up and knows that it will have to outrun the slowest gazelle, or it will starve to death. So in Africa, it doesn't matter if you are the lion or the gazelle. When that sun comes up, you had better be running."

The lion might not be able to run as fast as the cheetah, but when the sun comes up, the lion had better be ready to run. The gazelle might feel frustrated that it has to be ready to run each day

Figure 15.11 Each day the lion and the gazelle must be prepared to run if they want to survive another day.

Figure 15.12 If the lion and gazelle are not prepared to run each day, this becomes their fate.

A particular train of thought persisted in, be it good or bad, cannot fail to produce its results on the character and circumstances. A man cannot directly choose his circumstances, but he can choose his thoughts, and so indirectly, yet surely, shape his circumstances.

James Allen

The notion of turning the other cheek when slapped is most useful for the man doing the slapping, taking over the land, enslaving, and murdering the people.

Garland Sharp

or be eaten by lions. But, when the sun comes up the gazelle had better be ready to run. Neither the lion nor the gazelle has an excuse for not running. Regardless of racism, castes, class systems, or any feet on our neck, when the sun comes up we had better be prepared to run. If we perceive that neither the possibility nor probability exists for success at the time, we must stop blaming our circumstances, the system or other people, and be about the business of trying to make the possibility or probability exist.

As stated earlier, if we find it difficult or impossible to change our environment and circumstances, we can change our attitudes toward these. Although we cannot change our past, we can change our opinion of our past. This can be empowering for us. For example, a woman might adopt the belief that being raised poor is the reason she has low character and feels like a victim. In contrast, she might adopt the belief that being raised poor is the reason she has a strong character and can endure suffering. A person raised poor has this choice.

In the worst cases — when people live in ghettos or prison camps — it appears that they do not have choices. Yet, if we are unable to control the physical environment such as Viktor Frankl in the German concentration camp, we should not surrender what Frankl called the "last of human freedom." The last of human freedom was the freedom of individuals to choose their attitude in any situation, to choose their own way.

If we cannot change or control our physical environment or circumstances, we can control our attitude toward these as Frankl did. This helped him deal with the people in his environment who had their feet on his neck. Like Frankl, people have the power to visualize a better future while existing in their present situation. If we change our attitude toward present situations and visualize better situations, this will aid us in the re-socialization process.

Finally, how do we get the big foot of God off our neck? This might seem to be an insurmountable task. Through socialization, the ruling stratum uses things such as the church and the media to control our perception of God. The ruling stratum sometimes defines God as they choose. This acts in the same way as controlling the big foot of God. The ruling stratum **emphasizes** notions such as the divine rights of kings, outcasts being reincarnated into a higher caste, and rich men going to hell.

If people believe the rich man in the Bible died and went to hell and the poor man Lazarus died and went to heaven, they might mistakenly conclude that God prefers them to be poor. If they feel that people can be better Christians by being poor, they would probably move away from wealth. If the improvised outcasts in India believe that their status in life is the will of Brahma, Ganesha,

Krishna, or whoever the h... they believe is God at the time; they will probably remain outcasts.

If the outcasts believe that if they live a good life as an outcast, they will come back in the next life in a higher status, they will accept the reality presented to them. A higher status in their present life becomes a forbidden zone for them. We must remember that God did not create them to be outcasts or poor people. We must remember that they obtained their perception of God through socialization. Whether a black person in America, an outcast in India, or a poor white in England, most of what we believe about God was handed down to us. We obtained these beliefs through socialization.

If we take care of removing our foot from our neck, including realizing where our irrational perceptions of God came from, we should realize that God's foot is not on our neck. Our perception that God's foot is on our neck is just a form of our own foot being on our neck. We might need to change our perception of God. It is not God's will that **you** should be poor, lower class, or outcasts. People developed these ideas.

With the feet removed from our neck, we can shed our self-limiting beliefs and move to more empowered lives. After getting the feet off of our neck, we will probably experience a feeling of freedom. Now, we can work toward goals and objectives without working against ourselves. We might compare the feet on our neck to driving a car with the brakes on. Now that we have removed the feet and released the brakes, we can live more empowered lives. With the feet removed, we might now move into previously forbidden zones.

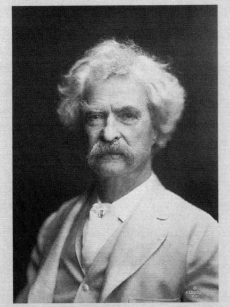

Figure 15.13 Mark Twain

In religion and politics, people's beliefs and convictions are in almost every case gotten at second hand, and without examination.
Mark Twain

We are no longer puppets being manipulated by outside powerful forces: we become the powerful force ourselves.

Leo Buscaglia

See, it's no in between: you're either free or you're a slave.

H. Rap Brown

Chapter 16

Entering the Forbidden Zone

I'd rather get my brains blown out in the wild than wait in terror at the slaughterhouse.
Craig Volk

Figure 16.1 White-tailed deer

People have a hard time letting go of their suffering. Out of a fear of the unknown, they prefer suffering that is familiar.

Thich Nhat Hanh

In the movie *"The Planet of the Apes"* as stated earlier, the apes in power defined the area where evidence existed that proved that humans once had superior societies to the apes ... as the "The Forbidden Zone." The fact that humans had superior societies would challenge the current society's established beliefs. The ideas of the Forbidden Zone and humans always being inferior to apes, persisted partly because the apes in power controlled the resources necessary to maintain those beliefs. The apes in power controlled resources such as the science, religion, and government which supported the notion that humans were and had always been inferior. The apes in power also had the power to punish those who entered the Forbidden Zone. The masses of apes' fear of the Forbidden Zone and their fear of punishment aided in keeping them from entering the Forbidden Zone.

Forbidden zones exist for such people as America's poor, England's lower class, and India's outcasts. What are these forbidden zones? Where are people forbidden to go? Where would they fall off the edge of the earth? The forbidden zone might be a person living in a certain neighborhood or becoming a scientist if they are from a lower caste or class. The forbidden zone might be a certain position in the company or government. The forbidden zone might be a marriage to people of a different color or a marriage outside of their class or caste. People have created these forbidden zones to maintain stratification.

As Robertson states, most of the social controls do not have to be administered externally. We conform to these controls without much questioning. We internalize the rules or norms of the society. The society socializes us to believe in and avoid forbidden zones. The environment then continues to reinforce these beliefs. This maintains the general belief throughout the society that the social order is natural and right. Individuals settle into comfort zones based on their beliefs. If they move out of their comfort zones and move toward the forbidden zones, they feel uncomfortable or stressed. Stress causes many individuals to move back into their comfort zone.

We keep ourselves out of forbidden zones — in part, based on internalized beliefs. This aids in maintaining stratification. For example, in many cases, our internalized beliefs about God determine our forbidden zones. If we believe that marrying a person of another skin color goes against the will of God, that marriage might be a forbidden zone. If we believe that rich people have the higher probability of going to hell as compared to poor people, being rich might be a forbidden zone.

We also avoid forbidden zones because of external rewards and punishments. We might receive rewards when we avoid the forbidden zones. These rewards might come in the form of positive feedback from the environment reinforcing the behavior. For example, everyone might be happy when we marry within our race, class, or caste. We receive rewards and positive feedback when we maintain the status quo and avoid forbidden zones.

In contrast, we might receive punishment when we enter forbidden zones. For example, group members might be dissatisfied when individuals marry outside their race, class, or caste and ostracize the couples. Even as recently as 1967 in America, in many states, a black person marrying a white person would have been guilty of breaking the law. As in the Planet of the Apes, the ruling stratum would punish individuals who entered the Forbidden Zone. Therefore, people's internal beliefs, the big lie, coupled with their external fears of punishment, the big stick, keep them out of the forbidden zones.

For some of us, entering forbidden zones might seem insurmountable. However, as with success, if one other person has entered and successfully lived in the forbidden zone, the possibility exists for others to do the same. It is acceptable for them to be rich. It is acceptable for them to marry a person of another mythical race, class, or caste. It is acceptable for blacks to play Major League Baseball or play quarterback in the National Football League. Blacks have found these to be forbidden zones in the past. Now, we might enter the forbidden zones of being rich, educated, or famous ... or whatever we desire.

As with any goal, even if no one else has entered and successfully lived in that forbidden zone, the possibility still might exist. Some forbidden zones exist for the individual, such as being the heavyweight boxing champion of the world, but not for groups of individuals based on race, class, or caste. Therefore, our forbidden zones should be examined — as with any truth. If we desire entry into a forbidden zone and find that the forbidden zone is truly forbidden — based on our critical evaluation — then we should avoid this area. If we find that the forbidden zone has been made forbidden by disempowering individuals, or by our self-limiting beliefs, we should simply close our eyes and jump.

Whatever you fear most has no power—it is your fear that has the power.
Oprah Winfrey

If we find the forbidden zone truly forbidden, then we should avoid this area. If we find the forbidden zone has been made forbidden by disempowering people or our self-limiting beliefs, we should close our eyes and jump.

Garland Sharp

Chapter 17

Goals—The Pathway to Change

The Sky's not the Limit.
Neil Degrasse Tyson

Success is measured by the size of the obstacles you had to overcome to reach your
GOALS

Figure 17.1 We might not agree with Brian Tracy that "success equal goals and all else is commentary." Yet, we know the importance of goals.

If you don't have a goal, any road will do.
Charles Tart

If you take the high road, it will be less crowded.
Rob Schriver

After getting the feet off our necks and realizing the fallacy of the forbidden zones, we can work more effectively to bring about change. We might not agree with Brian Tracy's statement, "that success equal goals and all else is commentary." Yet, we probably realize the importance of goals if we want to produce change and achieve objectives. The following is not an exhaustive treatise on the subject of goals, but a set of general guidelines for setting and achieving goals. Goals can be defined as specific objectives which a person wants to accomplish. Through introspection, we should define ourselves and our world. We should then create specific written goals to bring about and maintain desired conditions. Our goals should cause positive change in ourselves and others.

We should decide on and pursue goals which bring fulfillment and peace of mind. We get a feeling of accomplishment when we accomplish a task or goal. We have what Maxwell Maltz calls that "winning feeling" when we accomplish a worthwhile goal such as buying a house or getting a degree. Hopefully, we would not be fulfilled, nor get that winning feeling by being a contract killer, drug dealer, or pimp — no matter how much money we made.

We should ensure that our goals — when obtained — do not create the "so what" feeling, but that winning feeling. In the book *Think and Grow Rich*, Napoleon Hill tells a story of a man who spent years teaching an elephant to walk backward. Advertisements to the public invited them to come and see one of the great marvels of modern times. However, the animal walking backward failed to impress the people who filled the stands. So what if an animal walked backward?

A similar thing happened to one of your author's friends. The friend spent years trying to convince his girlfriend to have sex with him, without success. Years later, after they both married other people, he convinced her to commit adultery with him. He later told your author that when finished they just stopped and looked at each other — like saying "so what." He stated that they never had sex again. This illustrates having the wrong goal and getting that "so what" feeling when we accomplish that goal. It illustrates the ladder of success leaning on the wrong wall.

We should ensure that our goals bring fulfillment. For example, a woman could make big money in a profession chosen for her by her parents, and she finds the profession undesirable. If she fails to follow her dreams and live by her own values, she could be quite successful in societal terms — but still, at the end of her life have that "so what" feeling. Anyone who has read this far in this book probably would find little happiness after reaching the goal of being a highly successful drug dealer or pimp. Therefore, we should decide on definitions of ourselves and our world which we can be proud of

I used to work at The International House of Pancakes. It was a dream, and I made it happen.

Paula Poundstone

I gave my life to become the person I am right now. Was it worth it?

Richard Bach

I usually say I did the best I could with what I had. I have no major regrets.

Stokely Carmichael

What we're saying today is that you're either part of the solution, or you're part of the problem.

Eldridge Cleaver

and which bring fulfillment. We should ensure that our defined "self" aligns with our values. We should choose activities which lead to a fulfilled self and avoid the "so what" feeling when completing our goals.

Regardless, if we believe in reincarnation, heaven, or death being the final destination, we know that we only live this present life once. Therefore, we should make the best of our present life. Goals can help us avoid what might be called the Methuselah Complex. The Bible states many things about Moses, Joshua, Samson, and others. However, it only states that Methuselah lived 969 years, had children, and died.

It appears that Methuselah had no significant achievements worth writing about. We should avoid the Methuselah Complex, living our entire life without making any significant contribution to the world. We should desire that more be said about us than that we lived, had children, and died. Therefore, to avoid the "so what" feeling and Methuselah Complex, we — through introspection, should pursue goals which bring fulfillment and peace of mind for ourselves as well as others. Although these goals might have nothing to do with material success, we should strive to improve ourselves and make the world a better place.

Figure 17.2 Hopefully, this person did not live "down" to the name.

Death is more universal than life; everyone dies, but not everyone lives.
Sachs

Do not fear death so much, but rather the inadequate life.
Bertolt Brecht

A man's mind may be likened to a garden, which may be intelligently cultivated or allowed to run wild; but whether cultivated or neglected, it must, and will, bring forth.

James Allen

Figure 17.3 Two gardens, one cultivated and one running wild. But as James Allen said, whether cultivated or neglected the garden will bring forth.

In the absence of clearly defined goals, we become strangely loyal to performing daily trivia until ultimately we become enslaved by it.

Robert Heinlein

Maxwell Maltz, in his book entitled *Psycho-Cybernetics,* states that man is a goal striver. We appear to be the happiest when striving to achieve goals and planned tasks. We appear to be as happy working on a goal as actually obtaining the goal. Therefore, we should enjoy the process. Goal striving not only provides us with feelings of happiness but enables us to focus on desired results.

Earl Nightingale in the recording, the *Strangest Secret*, states that "We become what we think about." Goals help us to think about and focus on desired results. Goals aid us in controlling our thinking, keeping our minds on what we desire and off of what we do not desire. If we focus on our goals, we can adopt truths and actions that lead to accomplishing these goals. With goals, we might remain focused and better utilize our time.

In the book entitled, *As a Man Thinketh*, James Allen states that aimlessness is a vice. Therefore, we should remain focused on desired tasks and results — utilizing our time wisely. When performing tasks, we should constantly ask if the tasks are the best use of our time. We should align our thoughts, actions, and time with our desired results.

A woman might be very busy and tired but accomplish nothing meaningful that moves her toward her goals. She should work on things that empower and bring fulfillment, not on a thousand trivial things. If she neglects to focus and use her time wisely, other people will find ways to use her time. For example, when one of the author's family members stopped working in the workplace and became a housewife, other people wanted to use her time. Relatives and friends asked her to watch their kids. Her other family members asked her to return to West Tennessee to take care of various business activities.

If we do not plan our time, others might fill our schedule. The tasks from others seldom move us toward our goals. If allowed, those who lack direction can keep us from pursuing our goals.

We might go in circles and say that we have been somewhere. We might spend the whole day with our feet in the water and say that we have been swimming. We failed to reach our destination — or failed to go swimming. If we desire a certain destination, going in circles provides little help. If we chose to swim, putting our feet in the water accomplishes little. If our goal is getting to a certain destination, each step should lead to that destination. If swimming is the objective, putting our feet in the water should lead to further actions. We can be very busy and tired but get little accomplished toward achieving our goals.

My philosophy is that not only are you responsible for your life, but doing the best at this moment puts you in the best place for the next moment.

Oprah Winfrey

Figure 17.4 Defiance. We might need to decide what we will no longer take.

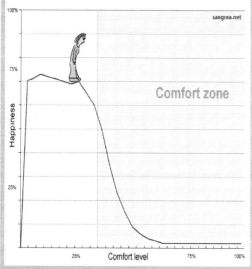

Figure 17.5 Comfort level vs. Happiness. As your comfort level increases, your happiness might go down.

Some of us become successful without written goals, but we would probably be more successful with written goals. We should define success for ourselves based on our purpose and values. Then, we might use goals — or more specifically, written goals — to close the gap between what is and what is desired. Goals provide us with the dissonance between the way things are and what is desired, causing us to have the urge to act. We act to remove the dissonance. We should examine what we will no longer accept and create goals to move to what is desired.

In the movie entitled *A Gathering of Old Black Men*, a black field worker had been beaten by white men all of his life. However, when he turned forty, he declared himself a man. He decided he would no longer take a beating. When a white man tried to beat him, the field worker hit and later killed the white man. We might need to decide that we will no longer take a beating.

We need to develop standards of what we will and will not accept, then set goals based on those standards. The standards should include time limits for reaching the goal. For example, if a woman decides that she will no longer accept being broke, the standard would be a certain level of income or wealth by a specific date. If she decides that she will no longer accept being 100 pounds overweight, the standard would be weighing 100 pounds less on a specific date. The standard provides feedback to her. Just as a report card in school provides feedback, we need feedback to determine our progress.

Myers corroborates this notion. He states that researchers found in many studies that "specific, challenging goals have motivated higher achievement, especially when combined with progress reports." If we make none or little progress, the feedback makes our comfort zone uncomfortable. As stated earlier, people move from pain to pleasure. The stress that results from the feedback provides the uncomfortable feeling in our old comfort zone. The old comfort zone now becomes the uncomfortable zone, causing us to move toward new levels of comfort. Once we reach more empowering comfort zones, we need to continue setting goals to reach even more empowering comfort zones. As with lifelong learning, we should believe in lifelong growth.

And the day came when the risk to remain tight in a bud was more painful than the risk it took to blossom.

Anais Nin

Photo Caption

Avoid having your ego so close to your position that when your position falls, your ego goes with it.

Colin Powell

If you want a quality, act as if you already had it. Try the "as if" technique. **William James**

Act as if it were impossible to fail.

Dorothea Brande

We should set goals in the different areas of our lives such as career, family, and personal. We should avoid having goals in only one area of our lives. For example, if we only have goals on the job and we lose the job, we might be headed for trouble. This appears to be one of the reasons many people die shortly after retirement. One of the author's colleagues was fired from his job. Shortly after being fired, the colleague died suddenly of a heart attack while leaving work in his car. Would he have died at that time if he had not received the news of being fired? There is no way of knowing. However, one thing is sure, if he had been looking forward to retirement and saw the event as positive instead of negative, his chances of living longer would have been greater.

It appears that the people who retire who have many interests live the longest. Therefore, we should have short and long-term goals for the different areas of our life. These might range from daily to-do lists to lifetime goals. As discussed earlier, our purposes and values should form the basis for our goals. We have to determine our purposes and values for ourselves to avoid that "so what" feeling.

To enhance our ability to achieve our goals, we might post pictures of the goals so that the goals can be seen daily. If we want a new car, we might put a picture of the new car on the wall in our office. If we want to lose weight, we might put a picture of ourselves when we weighed the ideal weight on our wall.

We also might begin to act as the desired person or act as if the desired goal has been achieved. If we cannot become the desired person immediately, we can become that person in our mind and act as if we are that desired person. For example, if a woman is 100 pounds overweight, she would not lose the weight immediately simply by redefining herself and taking on the role of a thinner person. However, she could act and visualize herself as the thinner person even before she loses the weight. If we want to be more confident, we should act and visualize ourselves as more confident.

We might also repeat positive affirmations to ourselves to enhance our ability to achieve our goals. As discussed earlier, if people tell the big lie long enough, they start to believe the lie. They can use the notion of telling the big lie long enough to facilitate change and growth. We can tell ourselves the desired "truth" long enough, and we will start to believe the "truth." If we desire to be more confident, we might frequently repeat to ourselves that we are confident.

Words are a form of action capable of influencing change.
Ingrid Bengis

As observed earlier, we might use visualization to enhance our ability to achieve our goals and de-hypnotize ourselves. Visualization appears to be one of the most powerful tools for change. It fails to cure all, but it certainly aids people in invoking change. Research strongly suggests that visualization enhances the individual's performance and ability to reach desired outcomes.

Myers in his book entitled "Psychology" cites the example where critics believed pianist Liu Chi Kung to be a better musician after imprisonment for seven years without practicing the piano. Liu Chi Kung attributed his continued development without physically practicing to rehearsing each note in his mind daily. Thomas Whetstone, a professor at the University of Louisville, supports the notion that visualization or mental practice enhances performance. In a study conducted by Whetstone with law enforcement officers, a group using mental practice scored significantly higher in marksmanship than a group that used no mental practice.

With visualization, we can vividly imagine things in our minds, causing our bodies to react to the imagined things as real. For example, if a man vividly imagines biting into a lemon, he feels the sensations in the body as if he had bitten into a real lemon. The body tends to react to things that we vividly imagine as real, especially when they invoke feelings or emotions. We have the same feelings or emotions which we would have if the thing or event was happening or had happened. We know this already, from experience.

If we vividly imagined having sex, we might become sexually aroused. We visualize and our bodies react all of the time when we worry. We might worry over something, visualizing it in our mind, and feel pain because of the worry. We might lose sleep or get ulcers over something imagined. For example, if a woman has an important job interview or an exam on the next day that she feels she has not adequately prepared for, she might be unable to sleep the night before. She might see herself doing poorly in her mind. If a person constantly has anxiety and worry about a loved one being killed in a war, the loved one might never get killed, but the imagined event could make the worried person sick.

We might react to a real or imagined event in much the same way. Imagined events might cause our hands to sweat and our heart to beat faster. For example, if a man feared snakes and imagined he saw a snake, he could become afraid. He would probably run and scream with fear. He reacts the same to a real or imagined snake.

What we vividly imagine powerfully influences our actions. As discussed earlier, if we imagine or visualize something with emotion, our bodies tend to react to the thing as if it were real. Therefore, we should persistently visualize our goal with emotions, until our goals are successfully completed. We should visualize the goal

Imagination is the beginning of creation. You imagine what you desire; you will what you imagine and at last you create what you will.

George Bernard Shaw

Figure 17.6 If we visualize falling off the edge of the earth, we will see the world through this perspective. We will avoid sailing too far out into the ocean.

One doesn't discover new lands without consenting to lose sight of the shore for a very long time.

Andre Paul Guillaume Gide

Imagination sets the goal picture, which our automatic mechanism works on. We act, or fail to act, not because of will, as is so commonly believed, but because of imagination.
Maxwell Maltz

being completed and feel the feeling we would feel if the goal **was** completed. In contrast, if we visualize failure, we might not try to accomplish our goals — or if we try, we might only give a half-hearted effort. If we visualize forbidden zones, we avoid the forbidden zones. If we visualize falling off the edge of the earth, we avoid sailing too far out in the ocean. We might use the power of visualization to enable or disable ourselves.

We should constantly visualize our goals successfully completed, in a relaxed state, and feel the feelings we would feel if the goals were completed. For example, when preparing to make a speech, for the best results, we should get ourselves in a relaxed state before visualizing. We might achieve this by counting backward and relaxing as we count down. We might take deep breaths and count backward down from ten to negative ten. Each time, we feel a bit more relaxed as we count backward and exhale deeply with each number. When relaxed, we should visualize making a successful speech.

To make the visualization of the event seem more real, we should not see our entire body as viewed by the audience, but we should visualize what we would see if giving the speech. In our mind, we should see, hear, and feel the things which we would experience if giving the speech. We might see the audience receiving the speech positively and the audience giving a standing ovation when we finish. We should feel the feelings which we would feel after giving a successful speech. However, if we find it difficult to visualize without seeing our whole body, we should still visualize. Also, we should not only visualize the desired results; we should visualize successfully preparing for the event. For example, we would not only visualize and feel the feelings which we would feel when making a successful speech but also visualize successfully preparing the speech. If writing a book, we would not only visualize and feel the feelings we would feel when the book appears on the New York Times Best Seller List, but also visualize successfully writing the book.

If we want to know more about visualization, any good book on success will probably have a section on visualization to enhance performance. Classics such as Brian Tracy's *Maximum Achievement*, Napoleon Hill's *Think and Grow Rich,* David Schwartz's *The Magic of Thinking Big*, and Maxwell Maltz's *Psycho-Cybernetics* include sections on visualization and mental practice.

Individuals might use visualization along with affirmations to enhance their ability to reach their goals. A technique taught in the course *Investment in Excellence* by Lou Tice used index cards for affirming and visualizing goals. In this technique, individuals write their goals in affirmation form on index cards. They write the goal as an affirmation as if they had already accomplished the goal. They then relax, read the affirmation and visualize the goal as accomplished. As they visualize the goal accomplished, they feel the feelings that they would feel if they had already accomplished the goal. The following template might help in writing affirmations.

> *Because of ...*
>
> *I am ...*
>
> *This makes me feel ...*
>
> For example, one might write, "Because of my persistence and excellent writing skills, I am a best-selling author, and this makes me feel extremely proud."

If a man wants to be a best-selling author, he writes the affirmation as if he **was** the best-selling author. In the relaxed state, he reads the affirmation, visualizes himself being the best-selling author, and feels the feeling he would feel if he were that author. He might visualize himself holding the New York Times Best Seller List that includes his book and feeling very proud. He might visualize himself at a book signing. He should visualize what he would see, hear, smell, taste, and feel at the book signing. He should feel all of the positive emotions he would feel if the event was happening.

Instead of counting backward down to a relaxed state, in his book entitled, *Think and Grow Rich,* Napoleon Hill suggests that individuals use affirmations and visualization upon awakening in the morning and just before falling asleep at night. In either case, whether counting down to relax or using Hill's technique, when visualizing, we should see and feel as if we already possess the goal.

We move toward or become what we constantly think about. Writing goals, acting as if, posting pictures, affirming, and visualizing, all can aid us in controlling what we constantly think about. These enable our reticular activating system (RAS) to aid us in achieving our goals. Without goals, we might have a scotoma for the things required for success.

Earl Nightingale said, "Success is when preparation meets opportunity, and opportunity is there all of the time." The RAS aids people in preparing for and seeing opportunities. The RAS will detect the things required for success or failure, based on what we constantly think about. Therefore, we should allow the RAS to work in empowering ways. For example, if we want to buy a house, we might write down all the things we want in the house. Then we might use affirmations and visualization to find the desired house. This technique helped the Sharp family to find and purchase a much-loved house quickly. When developing the list, the house was not on the market.

I know for sure that what we dwell on is who we become.

Oprah Winfrey

Figure 17.7 Walter Cronkite.
He would end the evening news with,
"And that's the way it is."

Pain is inevitable;
suffering is optional.
Unknown

Figure 17.8 Henry David Thoreau

However, shortly after developing the list, the seller coincidentally decided to sell the house. Writing what we want, as in this case, causes us to focus, and allows the RAS to find the things required for success.

Finally, achieving goals comes easier for us if we can control our environment by choosing things such as our neighborhood, peers, schools, and profession. Although many people make these choices, others find themselves trapped in prisons, ghettos, and castes. If trapped, they have to accept the status for the present time. As Walter Cronkite used to say after reporting the weekday news each evening, "And that's the way it is." As discussed earlier, after accepting the status, we should determine the gap between what exists and what we desire. Then, we can make things better by changing ourselves and our environment, or control our attitude towards our environment.

Although we cannot always control our environment, we can control our thoughts about the environment. We cannot always control our truth, but we can control our reaction to our truth. If we find ourselves trapped in places such as prisons, ghettos, or castes, we might control our reactions by trying to keep our thinking and attitude calm and cheerful while focusing on what we desire. Goals and visualization aid us in controlling our thoughts about the environment even when we cannot escape or change the environment. While in the concentration camp, Frankl visualized himself being free and making speeches regarding the horrors of the concentration camp. We should visualize ourselves coping successfully with the present problem while visualizing a better future. Therefore, change and growth are possible even in a ghetto, a concentration camp, or in an outcast status.

If one advances confidently in the direction of his dreams, and endeavors to live the life which he imaged, he will meet with success unexpected in common hours.

Henry David Thoreau

It's choice — not chance — that determines your destiny.

Jean Nidetch

The philosophers have only interpreted the world in various ways; the point, however, is to change it.

Karl Marx

If people such as Viktor Frankl and Nelson Mandela seem to have grown after their prison ordeal, the average person reading this book has a poor excuse for failing to redefine self and growing as a person. If people fail to define themselves, someone else will define them. If they fail to set goals, someone else will set goals for them. If they are content with someone else defining them and setting goals for them, that is fine. However, many of us want more from life. We want to live closer to our true potential. Again, we might not agree with Tracy that success equals goals, and all else is commentary, but written goals along with such activities as acting as if, using affirmations, and visualizing seem vital to extraordinary success.

Yes, you can think yourself out of a bad situation.

John Mason, a true friend of the Author.

Chapter 18

Stress: The Pull of the Comfort Zone

Figure 18.1 Sometimes the stress of modern life can be overwhelming.

The gem cannot be polished without friction, nor man perfected without trials.

Chinese Proverb

Between stimulus and response, there is a space. In that space lies our freedom and power to choose our response. In our response lies our growth and freedom.

Viktor Frankl

This chapter contains a brief treatise on the subject of stress, with general ideas on how to handle stress as we change. As we close the gap between what exists and what we want, stress might well occur. As we change and grow, the feedback from the environment, if allowed in, could cause stress. Whether we perceive it as positive or negative, change can cause stress. As we move from our comfort zones, this stress might cause us to feel very uncomfortable. We might then move back into our old comfort zones. Each time we move to a bigger house, obtain a better job, or have children, we might encounter significant stress.

Even these positive events in our lives can cause stress. For example, if a woman moves to a different job with greater responsibilities, the new environment in which she finds herself might cause stress. If she gets married, a good thing for most people, this could cause her to feel additional stress. Therefore, it seems that stress exists as a part of life, and most of us have some noteworthy stress from perceived positive and negative events.

When we are growing, how can we deal with the stress and avoid moving back into our old comfort zones? We need to understand what causes stress. In most cases an event fails to cause the stress; instead, it is our interpretation and reaction to the event that causes the stress. What causes stress for one person might fail to cause stress for another.

Here lies one of the keys to understanding and dealing with stress. If an encountered situation fails to cause stress for every person faced with that situation, then we must conclude that our reaction to the situation causes the stress rather than the situation itself. For example, a man talking with his boss might involve stress. However, the boss's son having the same conversation with the boss might feel little or no stress. The boss does not cause the stress, but the man's reaction to talking with his boss causes the stress. Therefore, as we are recognizing, the event does not cause the stress, but the person's interpretation of and reactions to the event causes the stress.

We cannot always control events, but we can choose our interpretation and reaction to the events. As Frankl stated, individuals in the concentration camp had the last of human freedom. Even under those horrible conditions, they could choose their attitude; they could choose their own way. Knowing that we have the power to choose our reaction to events, this helps us to combat stress. Certainly, Frankl could not have chosen to walk out of the concentration camp, but he could choose his attitude in the camp. In addition, he did not have to stay in the camp. He could have chosen death, as many others did. Therefore, whether free or incarcerated, a man still has choices. He does not have to do anything but eventually die.

Ever look at a male lion in a zoo? Fresh meat on time, females supplied, no hunter to worry about—he's got it made, hasn't he? Then why does he look bored?

Robert Heinlein

Lion by luisrock62/morgueFile free photo

Figure 18.2 This lion would probably not be able to survive in the Jungle.

Indolence is a delightful but distressing state; we must be doing something to be happy.

Mahatma Gandhi

We are built to conquer environment, solve problems, achieve goals, and we find no real satisfaction or happiness in life without obstacles to conquer and goals to achieve.
Maxwell Maltz

Although we do not have to do anything but die, we might find it stressful because of things we perceive that we have to do. We feel that we have no choice but to do certain things. In some cases, this might appear true. If we choose to do a certain thing, such as stay alive, there are certain things that we have to do. Once we make a decision, some things have to be done to support the decision. If we choose to be doctors, there are certain things we have to do to support the decision of becoming and remaining doctors. Even then, we still have the choice to decide which of the many avenues we would take to become and remain a practicing physician. Although our choice or decision to do a certain thing creates "have-tos," we can choose to change the original decision, and the "have-tos" would no longer exist.

When we choose a goal or a course of action, the feedback from the environment reveals to us the gap between what exists and what we desire. As alluded to earlier, this creates stress and "have-tos" if we want to close the gap. It appears that having to do certain things benefits us. In a time of retirement, when we have the fewest "have-tos," many die shortly after they retire. This suggests that they might need goals that create "have-tos" in their lives.

It appears that we need to choose goals which create beneficial stress and "have-tos" in our lives which move us toward empowered lives. As we should view this stress as being beneficial, we should view these "have-tos" in our lives as being beneficial. We can use stress and "have-tos" to create changes in our lives. The self-imposed "have-tos" create what might be defined as **eustress** or good stress to spur us into action. We can have a sense of urgency about doing certain things, avoiding procrastination. The stress and the sense of urgency can cause us to accomplish a tremendous amount of productive work. The stress and the "have-tos" can cause us to move toward desired results. This moves us out of our old comfort zones.

We might need to redefine ourselves and our world and expand our comfort zones. Just as we should choose what we will no longer accept, we should choose new levels of comfort, such as high levels of health and wealth. We should use goals and visualization to bring these about. Then the stress and "have-tos" can cause us to move forward where we belong in new comfort zones, instead of moving back into old comfort zones. This beneficial stress and the associated "have-tos" cause people to feel uncomfortable with present conditions. The old comfort zones become uncomfortable, causing us to move toward new levels of comfort.

Our perceived lack of control might also cause stress. Therefore, we might use goals to direct our lives to help maintain control.

Having goals and keeping our minds focused on our goals helps us to combat stress. It appears that if we work toward positive goals, we can be reasonably happy no matter what else is going on in our lives. We should stay focused on goals, keeping our minds mostly in the present moment, living one day at a time.

> Take therefore no thought for the morrow; for the morrow shall take thought for the things of itself. Sufficient unto the day is the evil thereof.
>
> *Matthew 6:34*

Our lack of competency causes stress. Being competent in our job and other activities help us to deal effectively with stress. We should be lifelong learners, always learning and growing in all areas of our lives. We should find an occupation which we love. This allows us to have a better chance of being successful. Also, to combat stress, we can use mental and physical practice to become better at the many activities we perform. We might not be able to practice a new job physically, but we can practice the job or nearly anything mentally. Therefore, we can practice any new task in our mind and avoid being a novice. We can also practice routine tasks in our mind, to become excellent at those tasks.

Our perceived failure might cause stress. We might ask the question, what would we do if we were certain of success? There would be no failure. Well, what is failure? Different people might define failure differently. We need to define failure for ourselves. Tony Robbins, a self-help author and motivational speaker, states, "People should define failure in ways that make it difficult to fail." Robbins states that when he failed to get the desired results when attempting a task, he did not define it as a failure if he did his best — or learned something.

This seems to be a good way to define failure. People only fail when attempting a task ... if they fail to do their best, or they fail to learn something. Oprah Winfrey states, "It is not failure if you enjoyed the process." We might want to define a perceived failure as a learning event. When defining failure in these ways, it helps to eliminate much of the stress and makes it easier for us to succeed. We need to decide what we want, which creates the "have-tos," and then do the "have-tos" in a relaxed, free-flowing manner. We should just relax while working, doing one thing at a time, defining failure in ways that make it hard for us to fail.

Our lack of good health causes stress. We know the value of exercise and nutrition in combating stress and avoiding illness. Then, we

---

I don't believe in failure. It is not failure if you enjoyed the process.

Oprah Winfrey

Stressed – Faster Faster by Grea, Sangrea.net /CC-BY-ND-3.0

Easiness by Jorge.maturana, Wikimedia Commons/CC- BY-3.0.

Figure 18.3 Stress vs. Easiness. Stress can be overwhelming. We should choose easiness. We should relax and enjoy the process.

should have health goals to build healthy bodies to combat stress. Stress can cause us to become sick. Then, sickness can bring on more stress. To stop this vicious cycle and maintain good health, we might also find some stress reduction techniques helpful such as biofeedback or meditation. These have worked for many.

If all of this talk about stress and "have-tos" seems stressful, it does not have to be that way. We should just relax and enjoy the process, knowing that, in most cases, it is not the event that causes the stress but our interpretation and reaction to the event. To help fight stress, we need to choose empowering reactions to events — whether dealing with the boss or taking on new responsibilities. We might do this by simply deciding to change our interpretation and reaction to the event, or we might use affirmations and visualization to overcome the stress. If using affirmations and visualization, we should affirm and visualize ourselves acting and feeling relaxed in situations that normally cause stress. In summary, we should create new comfort zones and move up to these comfort zones while defining failure in ways that make it difficult for us to fail.

It was not a failure, but a learning event.

Garland Sharp

Chapter 19

Maintaining Continuous Growth and Success

Winning is a habit. Unfortunately, so is losing.

Vince Lombardi

Victories attained by right thought can only be maintained by watchfulness. Many give way when success is assured, and rapidly fall back into failure.

James Allen

Wise men profit more from fools than fools from wise men; for the wise men shun the mistakes of fools, but fools do not imitate the successes of the wise.

Cato the Elder

Figure 19.1 Learning. A diploma or degree should be just the beginning of lifelong learning.

This book deals with improving the human condition by individuals developing better ways of thinking and behaving. It centers on the notion that we can understand and improve the human condition. Therefore, we can improve ourselves and the world. After we have redefined ourselves and improved ourselves and the world, we need empowering habits for continuous growth and success.

We need to employ habits which successful people have. For example, if we define Oprah Winfrey as successful and want to achieve some of the things she has achieved, we should examine how she thinks and the habits that made her successful. We should examine and adopt some of the thinking, feeling, and behaving characteristics which led to her success. We might try to work for or with her and get to know her personally. Certainly, it would be great to have her as a mentor. If we cannot get to know her personally, we might get an idea of her TFB-characteristics by watching her on TV and reading her books. Although most of us cannot get to know anyone such as Winfrey personally, there is probably someone whom we do know who is successful whom we might obtain as our mentor.

Success equals goals, and all else is commentary — might not be true. However, we should realize that we should form the habit of utilizing goals along with the other success techniques such as acting as if, affirmations, and visualization for continuous growth and success. As discussed earlier, these appear to be essential for extraordinary success. Additionally, we might need to replace destructive habits such as worry, envy, and fear which impede growth ... with empowering habits such as acting confidently, wishing the best for others, and acting boldly to enhance growth.

Lifelong learning appears to be a key habit of successful people. We should form this habit for continuous growth and success. We should set up a research and development (R&D) program for ourselves. This R&D program should include lifelong learning. Lifelong learning comes from schools, books, travels, vocabulary building, and of course, doing. The knowledge obtained can aid in the continuous redefining of ourselves for growth and success. Therefore, we need a continuous flow of knowledge for constant growth and success which comes through studying and doing. It appears that the more we learn, the more we can do. Also, the more we do, the more we learn.

Learning is not compulsory — neither is survival.

W. Edwards Deming

> Change is the end result of all true learning.
>
> *Leo Buscaglia*

Figure 19.2 Hard Work. Sometimes to succeed we have to work hard. As Jim Rowan said, "if it is easy, do it easy. If it is hard, do it hard."

> You know you are on the road to success if you would do your job, and not be paid for it.
>
> *Oprah Winfrey*

> I never blame failure... there are too many complicated situations in life. But, I am absolutely merciless toward lack of effort.
>
> *F. Scott Fitzgerald*

No matter how much we learn, define ourselves, and set goals, we must be willing to take action to accomplish anything. We must **do** something. We should form the habit of getting things done. We have to work. Sometimes, we have to work hard. However, if we are doing something we love and moving toward desired goals, the work can be fun. Even if the work seems hard, if we are to succeed, we must do it anyhow. As Jim Rowan said, "If it is easy, do it easy. If it is hard, do it hard." Not only should we be involved in lifelong learning, but also involved in lifelong **doing** for continuous growth and success.

> The difficult we do immediately, the impossible might take a little longer.
>
> **Unknown**

The system for continuous growth and success includes the habit of doing what one loves, with excellence. Doing what we love appears to promote excellence. In turn, excellence at what we do can aid us in loving what we are doing. We should find work that we love, and try to become one of the best at what we are doing. We should enjoy our work. We will probably be good at what we love, and have a higher probability of doing it with excellence. The eustress or positive stress from doing what we love with excellence strengthens our chances of being healthier and living longer. Doing what we love and achieving excellence appears to raise our self-esteem. As our self-esteem rises, we might be able to do more and be more successful. As we become more successful, our self-esteem continues to rise. Therefore, we should love what we do and have the discipline and the perseverance to do what we love ... with excellence.

We need the habit of persistence. We must persist, and sometimes keep going when others have quit. For example, sometimes it takes discipline and persistence to obtain a job we can love. If a woman decides to become a physicist or chemist, it takes many years of study and work. If she likes what she is doing and has meaningful goals, she might not mind working when others have stopped. She might use rewards, goals, affirmations, and visualization to aid her in persisting. She might have rewards for herself at certain stages of accomplishment, and rewards at the completion of the goal. For example, when writing this book, rewards were established by the author at certain stages of the book.

The reward of having a fig newton after each writing session got the author into the habit of writing. After writing each draft, a reward such as a new pair of pants or a day off from work helped him to continue to write. The setting of goals and using affirmations also

Photo Caption

aided him in persisting. However, perhaps the most important thing done by the author which aided him in persisting was visualizing this book being successfully published ... before each writing session. Rewards, goals, affirmations, and visualization can aid us in persisting until successful actions become a habit.

The author grew up watching the cartoon where the coyote tried without success to catch the Road Runner. But, Figure 19.3 shows what could happen if we persist. The coyote — after years of trying — finally caught the Road Runner. Therefore, we should ensure that we persist in doing the tasks that bring success and happiness.

We should form the habit of utilizing our time effectively. To combat the factor which aids in maintaining stratification — spending most of our time on tasks to satisfy basic needs — we should set goals to move beyond activities required just to satisfy these needs. If we are to combat the factor that aids in maintaining stratification — after satisfying our basic needs, failing to utilize our time wisely to bring about change — we should continually ask ourselves what activities are the best use of our time ... and do those activities.

We should ensure that we use time wisely, and have goals aligned to avoid conflict between our goals, plus conflict between our goals and useless activities. For example, we should avoid goal conflict. If a man wants to become a priest, he might have to give up the goal of being a rock star. People should also avoid conflict between goals and useless activities. If they want to become physicists, they should avoid watching three hours of TV each night, spending time on nonproductive work, and hanging around friends who constantly tell them that they cannot become physicists. These fail to meet the standard of utilizing time wisely.

In utilizing our time effectively, we should look for catalysts which will propel us forward ... and form the habit of doing these tasks. For example, the long-term goal of obtaining a large sum of money and obtaining a degree are catalysts which could help us accomplish many smaller goals. Having plenty of money could achieve the goals of being debt free, buying a new car, and saving money for our kid's college. Therefore, instead of working on many smaller goals, we might work on the large goals which — when reached — will take care of the smaller goals, or empower us to take care of the smaller goals. We might consider the 80/20 Rule or the Pareto Principle named after Vilfredo Pareto.

The Pareto principle indicates that — of the activities performed by people — about 80% of the effects come from about 20% of the activities. If the principle is correct, then 20% of what we do will result in 80% of the results. About 80% of what they do will result in only about 20% of the results. Therefore, we should seek to do the

Drawn by Michija Sharp, your author's grandson.

Figure 19.3 Persistence. We should ensure that we persist in doing the tasks that bring success and happiness.

Keep away from people who try to belittle your ambitions. Small people always do that, but the really great make you feel that you, too, can become great.

Mark Twain

If you're not playing a big enough game, you'll screw up the game you're playing just to give yourself something to do.

John Ringer

Figure 19.4 Jack and Jill picture was taken from "The Book of Knowledge, The Children's Encyclopedia."

All work and no play might make Jack a rich man, Jill an unhappy wife, and then Jill, a rich widow.

Garland Sharp

20% that yields the 80% of the results. We should do the things which act as catalysts, propelling us towards the bigger goals.

We should form the habit of keeping our mind mostly in the present moment. As discussed earlier, only the present time exists. We exist in a single time and a single space. We can usually handle the present moment. Trying to handle and worry about the past, present, and future can be overwhelming for us. In the book entitled *How to Live 365 Days a Year*, John Schindler states that people should form the habit of keeping their thinking and attitudes calm and cheerful, right now. Not only should they keep their minds in the present moment, with their thinking and attitude calm and cheerful, they should also keep their minds on what they desire. In contrast, they should keep their minds off of what they do not desire.

As we develop the habits which contribute to continuous growth and success, we should also form the habit of resting, relaxing, and having fun. We should take the time to enjoy the journey. We should enjoy life now, being grateful that things are going as well as they are. We should reward ourselves for a job well done. Men should recognize that all work and no play can make Jack a rich man, Jill an unhappy wife, and then Jill, a rich widow.

If you have the choice to sit it out or dance, I hope you dance.

Lee Ann Womack

Figure 19.5 **Bobby and Helen Marable**. They love to dance.

Finally, as we know, in addition to the habits of success discussed in this chapter, we must form the habit of critical thinking to develop truths closer to real world objects/events. Because — if our life is built on falsity, what have we gained? We need to shed false

Figure 19.6 Ships were not built just to sit in the harbor. If they sail ships, the captains must not be afraid of sailing to the edge of the earth and falling off that edge.

A ship is safe in the harbor, but that's not what ships were built for.

William Shedd

No one would remember the Good Samaritan if he only had good intentions. He had money as well.

Margaret Thatcher

Figure 19.7 Painting of Lazarus by Fyodor Andreyevich Bronnikov. If on a road in America or England, you meet poor Lazarus of the Bible, "kill him."

consciousness and move beyond class consciousness to success consciousness. We should define ourselves and truths that empower us to have continuous growth and success.

We might have to discard definitions of ourselves and the world which society has presented to us. We should define a self whom we would be proud to have written about on our tombstone. We should ensure that our beliefs empower us. If we sail ships, we must not be afraid of sailing to the edge of the earth and falling off that edge.

We must rid ourselves of our forbidden zones whether we or others built these forbidden zones. We should continue to move toward established goals, even if this means entering forbidden zones. We should decide what we will no longer accept. We need to raise our standards. We need to go beyond the black field hand's decision of not taking a beating from the white man after turning forty, in the movie the *"A Gathering of Old Black Men."* We need to decide that we will never take a beating whether twenty, forty, or one hundred and forty.

We might need to develop comfort zones which make us feel comfortable with success and having plenty of money ... and uncomfortable without success and having little money. We need to raise our money consciousness and our comfort zone as related to money. Being around luxury and a positive environment seems to foster our creativity. We all have the same amount of time. Therefore, people should build wealth so that they can spend time creating instead of spending most of their time just surviving. If on a road in India they meet a cow, they should kill it. Not literally, but figuratively kill the cow and remove it from their consciousness. If on a road in America or England, they meet poor Lazarus of the Bible, they should figuratively kill him and remove him from their consciousness. The cow and Lazarus represent the false and poverty consciousness of millions of people. It is not God's will for **you** to be poor, and **you** will not come back as a cow. We should develop levels of wealth so that we can better control our time. Again, if we have wealth, we can spend our time creating instead of just surviving. We might believe that the poor will be on Earth always, but **you** do not have to be one of the poor.

Figure 19.8 A Cow in India. If on a road in India, one meets a cow, "kill it."

Chapter 20

Epilogue

Drawn by Charles Slay

Figure 20.1 Tearful Eye. Hopefully, the undertaker will be sorry when you die.

Let us so live that when we come to die, even the undertaker will be sorry.

Mark Twain

Figure 20.2 Mrs. Marie Sharp, your author's mother in prayer and Bible reading just before her death.
If our belief works well, we might keep our belief. Would we want to have taken the most cherished beliefs from this dear lady?

As you come to the end of this book, the greatest hope for the author is that it will have a positive effect on your life. Hopefully, you can truly say that reading this book became a defining moment in your life. As Robertson and Christian's books were for the author, maybe this book will be a reference book for your life. A sincere desire is that this book has changed, is changing, and will change your life for the better. Hopefully, you will evolve into a better person in part because of this book. Hopefully, this book builds up individuals instead of tearing them down. If it tears down the self-limiting beliefs that hold the individual down, it has served its purpose. If it helps tear down ideologies and systems such as racism, castes, and royalty, it has served its purpose. However, if our belief system works well, we might keep our beliefs. The purpose of this book is not to tear down all cherished beliefs, but to inspire individuals to critically think about beliefs or truths. Hopefully, it can be used in conjunction with truths that work best for each of us.

Today is the first day of the rest of your life, along with the other over seven billion people on earth. It is a great time to be alive. It all starts over today. Even when we encounter a learning event, or we do not live up to our expectations, we can start this day afresh. We cannot return to the past because the past does not exist. Yet, as the mythical Phoenix, consumed by fire, rises from the ashes to live again, we can start a new day today defining a self and a world we can be proud of, and then create that self and world. Remember, we are both the cause and the effect. We are the effect because of our hereditary blueprint, the inescapable conditions, and the environment. Yet, we are the cause because we can always change our mind and choose a different past — in effect. But, more importantly, we can change our thinking, feelings, and behaving characteristics and choose a different past, present, and future. Then, we can create a better present and a better future.

Yes, we can see that we are both the effect based on our hereditary blueprint, the inescapable conditions, and environment ... and we are greatly the cause of the effect based on our choices and actions. Therefore, we should choose and act well because we are the architects of our lives. Remember that if people can convince an outcast to become an outcast, and live his or her life as an outcast, then pass this status on to future generations, then we can convince ourselves of the opposite extreme of being super successful, and live our entire life as super successful — and then pass this status on to future generations.

Yes, we can!

Everyone

Photo Caption

So now as this book ends, farewell might be in order, and maybe one day your path might cross your author's path. But until then, as Truman stated when the Truman Show ended and he escaped from his disabling reality: "Good morning, good afternoon, good evening, and good night." It is now time for us to embrace a new reality of exploring better ways of being human.

Man has but to right himself to find that the universe is right; and during the process of putting himself right, he will find that as he alters his thoughts toward things and other people, things and other people will alter toward him.

James Allen

If people can convince an outcast to become an outcast, and live his or her life as an outcast, then pass this status on to future generations; then we can convince ourselves of the opposite extreme of being super successful, and live our entire life as super successful — and then pass this status on to future generations.

Garland Sharp

Keep the Faith, baby!

Many People

Ancient Model of History (Bernal)   The model of history that purports that the Greek culture had arisen because of colonization by black Egyptians and Phoenicians around 1500 B.C.

Aristocentrism   An unwarranted claim to superiority.

Aryan Model (Bernal)   The model of history taught in most schools today developed by Europeans during the first half of the 19th Century. According to the Aryan Model, there had been an invasion from the North that overwhelmed the local Aegean or pre-Hellenic culture. Greece civilization is seen as the result of the mixture of the Indo-European-speaking Hellenes and the indigenous subjects.

Belief perseverance   The tendency of people to cling to their beliefs even when they find the beliefs untrue.

Caste system   A closed form of stratification that divides the society into strata determined by birth and is usually permanent.

Class system   A form of stratification primarily based on economics or social status. In this system, individuals might move up or down in the system.

Class consciousness   Class consciousness is an ideology accepted by individuals that cause them to see the true nature of their plight as an oppressed group and question their social arrangement in the system.

Classical conditioning   A type of learning that occurs when a neutral stimulus produces a conditioned response.

Coherence-test   A truth-test where a fact/claim could be accepted as true if it harmonizes (coheres) with other facts that the individual has already accepted as true.

Comfort zone   The place or state where individuals feel comfortable.

Confirmation bias   The tendency for people to seek information that confirms their beliefs while overlooking information that conflicts with their beliefs.

Conventional wisdom   The prevailing beliefs of the society.

Correspondence-test   A truth-test that requires a person to check a fact-claim against a real object/event. If fact-claim corresponds to the real object/event, the person considers the fact/claim "true".

Critical thinking (Brooke Moore and Richard Parker)   The careful deliberate determination of whether we should accept, reject, or suspend judgment about a claim—and the degree of confidence with which we accept or reject the claim.

Cultural integration   The tendency for the different TFB-characteristics in a society to provide thinking, feeling, and behaviors that interact to hold the environment or society together.

Dearyanianized   To rid oneself of the beliefs that support caste systems developed by Aryans.

Decaucasinized   To rid oneself of the beliefs that support classism and racism developed by Caucasians.

Dehypnotized (Maltz)   Individuals overcoming being hypnotized by negative ideas they have accepted from others, or negative ideas they have repeated to themselves or convinced themselves are true.

Egocentric/selective detection   Individuals selecting only bits of what they are capable of observing to use for thinking.

Egocentric conditions   The condition humans have to face simply because of being human.

Egocentric fallacy   The belief by individuals that what they experience through their perceptual and information-processing equipment is exactly as the real world object/event or 100 % true.

Egocentric illusion   The belief by individuals that the entire universe revolves around them in a particular time and space. They believe they are the center of the universe.

Egocentric predicament (Perry)   The condition of individuals being trapped in their bodies and can only experience the World through their perception.

Egocentric trap   The condition that individuals find themselves trapped in a single time and a single space.

False consciousness   An ideology accepted by individuals that keep them from seeing the true nature of their plight and justifies their social arrangement in a system. They look for something outside of themselves and their oppressors as the cause of their plight.

Forbidden zones   Places where individuals are forbidden to go and things they are forbidden to do.

Genographic Project   A five-year effort to understand the human journey and where humans came from and how they got to where they live today conducted in collaboration with The National Geographic Society, IBM, geneticist Spencer Wells, and the Waitt Family Foundation.

Halo effect   When a quality exhibited by an individual influences our judgment of other qualities in that individual.

Hereditary blue print   Individuals' genes that aid in determining their physical and mental characteristics.

Human predicaments   The predicaments and inescapable conditions individuals face simply because of being human. Because of these conditions, individuals do not know all that is going on in the world.

Hypnotized (Maltz)   The same power over individuals as the hypnotist's words over a hypnotized subject caused by ideas the individuals have uncritically accepted from others, or ideas they have repeated to themselves or convinced themselves are true.

Illusory correlation   The belief that there is a correlation between events when no correlation exists.

Inescapable conditions   The conditions individuals face simply because of being human such as being trapped in a single time, space, and body. Also, the Reticular Activating System (RAS) allowing only essential information to be detected and perceived by the individual and the Subconscious Mind sometimes without being known by the individual, causes the individual to think, feel, and behave irrationally. Finally, many of the beliefs, based on limited information, held by the conscious mind limit the individual.

Institutionalized   The condition prisoners find themselves in after being incarcerated for long periods. They become more comfortable in prison than free in society as describes by a lady in Cookeville, Tennessee, who had a daughter who had been incarcerated for many years. The condition people find themselves in because of conditioning that causes them to remain trapped in undesirable conditions.

Jim Crow laws   Laws used after slavery to keep blacks segregated from whites and to keep blacks in the lower stratum.

Manifest Destiny   The belief by earlier Western settlers that it was their destiny to own the land in the western parts of the United States.

Methuselah complex   The notion of individuals living their entire life without making any significant contribution to the world.

Myth   A belief based on real or perceived real truths.

Myth (Religion) A "traditional story dealing with supernatural beings, ancestors, or heroes that informs or shapes the worldview of a people, as explaining aspects of the natural world or delineating the customs and ideals of society." as described in the American Heritage Dictionary. The traditional story may be defined as real and becomes real in its consequences. The story can then becomes religion.

Myth-makers Individuals that develop myths or beliefs.

Observational learning A primary way individuals form their TFB-characteristics and learn the ways of society. Through detection and perception, they learn from observing their environment, which includes observing others. Much of what they learn about self and the world come from observing and imitating others.

Operant conditioning The conditioning that occurs when the feedback from an act causes the individual to repeat or avoid the act.

Pareto Principle The principle named after Vilfredo Pareto. This principle indicates that of the activities performed by individuals; about 80% of the effects come from about 20 % of the activities.

Perceived real truths The truths that become real because people believe them to be real. For example, the belief or truth that witches cause illness.

Perception The process of individuals interpreting or decoding information.

Personality The general thinking, feeling, and behaving characteristics that are unique to the individual.

Pragmatic-test A truth-test where a fact/claim could be accepted as true if it works or brings about the desired results.

Racism The belief that one racial group is different from another and because of a false sense of superiority, feelings of inferiority, or the feelings of fear, unequal treatment is justified.

Real truths The truths that are true for everyone. For example, $2 + 2 = 4$ and the fact that gravity causes dropped objects to fall to the Earth are true for everyone whether they believe these true or not.

Real world objects/events The way things really are such as gravity causing objects to fall to the earth when the object is dropped.

Reticular Activating System (RAS) The part of the brain that filters information and allows essential information to be detected and perceived by the individual; limits what the individual experiences; and causes individuals to detect from their environment only the essential or relevant items to them at the time.

Scotomas (blind spots) A blind spot in psychological awareness.

Selective detection and biased perception (SDBP) The process of individuals selectively detecting and biasedly perceiving what is going on in the world.

Self The individuals' total being that includes their physical and mental components. In other words, the self would be one's distinctive way of being human.

Self-efficacy The belief of individuals in their ability to accomplish a task or become a certain way.

Self-esteem How individuals feel about themselves.

Self-image How individuals view themselves.

Self-limiting beliefs The beliefs that limit the individual.

Self-worth The feeling individuals have about their worthiness.

Sensation The process of transducers such as their eyes, nose, and ears detecting physical energy from the world then encoding it in the brain.

Simple causation Individuals believing that a single factor caused an effect instead of contributing factors.

Socialization The continuing process of social interaction whereby individuals acquire their thinking, feeling, behaving characteristics and learn how to be human.

Social Stratification A system used by a society to rank groups of people in a hierarchy. This system unequally stratifies people in that society.

Sociolosophy It is the critical analysis of human behavior by examining both the social sciences and philosophy to provide additional insight into how we develop, maintain, and change our thinking, feeling, and behavior in an attempt to devise better ways of being human.

"So what" feeling The feeling individuals get when they accomplish a goal or task that brings little or no fulfillment.

TFB-characteristics The thinking, feeling, and behaving characteristics, that forms the basis of the individual's personality.

Thomas Theorem (W. I. Thomas) If people define situations as real, they are real in their consequences.

Transducers Parts of the body such as the eyes, nose, and ears used to detect physical energy from the world that is encoded in the brain.

Truth Individuals' view of reality. The beliefs they have about themselves and the World.

Truth-tests Tests individuals might use to determine the truth of a fact/claim.

Allen, J. (2010). <u>As a Man Thinketh</u>. Hustonville, KY: Golgotha Press.

Bernal, M. (1987). <u>Black Athena, The Afroasiatic Root of Classical Civilization, Volume 1: The Fabrication of Ancient Greece 1785-1985</u>. New Brunswick, New Jersey: Rutgers University Press.

Bernal, M. (1991). <u>Black Athena, The Afroasiatic Root of Classical Civilization, Volume 2: The Archaeological and Documentary Evidence.</u> New Brunswick, New Jersey: Rutgers University Press.

Chomsky, N. (1993). <u>The Prosperous Few and the Restless Many</u>. Berkeley, California: Odonian Press.

Christian, J. L. (1994). <u>Philosophy, an Introduction to the Art of Wondering</u> (5th ed.). Fort Worth, Texas: Holt, Rinehart, and Winston.

Dawkins, R. (2006). <u>The God Delusion</u>. New York: A Mariner Book, Houghton Mifflin Company.

Descartes, R (1641). <u>Meditation I</u> [Online]. Available: http://en.wikipedia.org/wiki/Methodic doubt

Frankl, V. E. (1963). <u>Man's Search for Meaning</u> (2nd ed.). New York: Pocket Books.

Hill, N (1960). <u>Think and Grow Rich</u> (2nd ed.). New York: Fawcett Crest

Kwak, C. H. (2007). <u>New World Encyclopedia</u> [Online]. Available: http://www.newworldencyclopedia.org/entry/Inquisition.

Maltz, M. (1960). <u>Psycho-cybernetics. A New Way to Get More Living Out of Life.</u> New York: Prentice-Hall.

Montagu, A. (1964). <u>Man's Most Dangerous Myth, the Fallacy of Race</u> (4th ed.). New York: The World Publishing Company.

Moore, B. N. & Parker, R. (2001). <u>Critical Thinking</u> (6th ed.). New York: McGraw-Hill.

Myers, D. G. (2001). <u>Psychology</u> (6th ed.). New York: Worth Publishers.

Nightingale, E. (2013). <u>The Strangest Secret</u>. Seaside, Oregon: Watchmaker Publishing.

Pickett J. P. (Ed.). (2007). <u>The American Heritage College Dictionary</u> (4th ed.). New York: Houghton Mifflin Company.

Robertson, I. (1987). <u>Sociology</u> (3rd ed.). New York: Worth Publishing.

Schindler, J. A. (1970). <u>How to Live 365 Days a Year</u>. New York: Fawcett World Library.

Sharp, G. (2001). <u>The Relationship among Self-esteem, Self-Efficacy, and Training performance at a Government-funded Nuclear Operations Complex in East Tennessee.</u> Unpublished master's thesis, University of Tennessee, Knoxville.

Shemer, M. (1999), <u>How We Believe: The Search for God in an Age of Science.</u> New York: W.H. Freeman and Company.

Smedley. A. (2003). <u>Race the Power of an Illusion</u> [Online]. Available: http://www.pbs.org/race/000 About/002 04-experts-02-01.htm.

Tracy, B. (1995). <u>Maximum Achievement</u>. New York: Simon & Schuster.

Welsing, F. C. (2004). <u>The Isis (Yssis) Papers: The Keys to the Colors</u>. New York: C.W. Publishing.

Whetstone, T. S. (1995). Enhancing psychomotor skill development through the use of mental practice. Journal of Industrial Teacher Education [Online]. Available: http://scholar.lib.vt.edu/ejournals/JITE/v32n4/whetstone.html.

Woodson, C. G. (2013) <u>The Mis-Education of the Negro.</u> New York: Start Publishing.